PERILOUS ESCAPE

PERILOUS ESCAPE

My Journey From Nazi Europe
to Freedom

§

AN AUTOBIOGRAPHY

By

Dr. Chaskel Wyszkowski

Edited by
Dr. Richard White

URIM PUBLICATIONS
Jerusalem • New York

Perilous Escape
My Journey From Nazi Europe to Freedom
An Autobiography
by Chaskel Wyszkowski

Typeset by Ariel Walden

Printed in U.S.A.

First Edition

ISBN 978-1-60280-351-0

Urim Publications
P.O. Box 52287,
Jerusalem 9152102 Israel
www.UrimPublications.com

Library of Congress Cataloging-in-Publication Data in progress.

This autobiography
Is
Dedicated to the memory of

CHAVA, *a"h*

My beloved wife
And to the many wonderful years
We shared together.

Contents

Introduction

CHILDHOOD, ADULTHOOD, and old age are by and large three phases in a person's life that are governed by time. This order of human development, however, is often disrupted and thrown into chaos when impacted by some explosive earth-shattering event.

My childhood was cut short, and adulthood rapidly upstaged it. Perhaps this reflected a condition prevalent during World War II among those of my age who managed a quick escape to safety. We were in desperate flight once Europe was engulfed by throat-cutting, inhuman madmen with German, Ukrainian, Lithuanian, and other faces thirsty for Jewish blood.

From that desperation, punctured by the mass tragedy of millions of physically and spiritually broken Jewish lives, the catalyst for an entirely new Jewish world emerged in one major leap. With renewed G-d-endowed energy and optimism, we began to reconstruct our lives to even greater heights. Jewish pride and prominence, a Jewish state, a resurgence of yeshivas together with some of their imposing Torah giants, and a major reshaping of Jewish demography around the world were the results of that new breath of life. Jewish Europe after the Holocaust is dead or dying and much of the same can be said of the majority of Jewish communities in the Arab world. That evolution gave rise to two large dynamic communities in Israel and the United States. Many of us chose to enjoy both of these worlds.

The sharp contrast between my early and later years can be measured by the differences between involuntary desperate adventures versus voluntary trips in later life.

My story begins with a lonely journey together with my father into the unknown world. We left behind us nothing but tragedy; my mother, brother, grandfather, uncles, aunts and friends were never to be seen again. With G-d's help my story ends with three amazing children, many wonderful grandchildren and beautiful great grandchildren. This is our response to Hitlers around the globe. My children and their offspring have chosen a path in Jewish life that brings honor to their past and great hopes for the future. Ever since our escape, I have tried, largely on my own, to explore the renewed Jewish world, in Australia, Israel, and the United States. An account of the search and experience, which gradually made me part of this world, is the substance of this book.

Early on, I came to the recognition that the cornerstone for a healthy and secure Jewish future consists of three vital elements: love of Israel, strong family-centered living, and education; in other words, Torah and *Derech Eretz* (worldliness). Our rejuvenated mental state in the post-Holocaust era, has helped trigger the ambition to do everything possible to maximize these goals. With this vision in mind, my family and I continue to passionately head in this direction. Much of this sentiment is reflected in the pages of this story.

I never kept diaries, nor did I ever contemplate writing this story. But now that I did, I hope that the reader and especially my own family, children, grandchildren, and ultimately great grandchildren, who are constantly in my thoughts, will gain some personal insight into the incredible events, and into the men and women who are all the backbone of this book.

In conclusion, I wish to express my deep appreciation for the timely comments and observations of my dear daughters Malka Treuhaft and Varda Neuhaus, as well as of my dear son Aaron Dovid Wyszkowski.

I am especially most grateful to my beloved grandson Dovid Neuhaus, without whom many historical pictures and documents might have never seen the light of day. His time-consuming and painstaking efforts in searching out information and help in decipherment of numerous sources, including information on family members who are no longer with us, as well as his masterful work with photography deserve a place of honor in my story.

Many thanks to all my grandchildren and great grandchildren, without whom this story would have remained incomplete.

I also wish to express my deep appreciation to Moshe Rosenblum of Toronto, Canada, for his assistance in the translation of my mother's thirty important, heart-rending Polish letters from the Warsaw Ghetto, which have a prominent place in this book. My dear wife Chava, *a"h*, and I became friends with Rochelle and Moshe Rosenblum during our winter stays in Century Village, Deerfield Beach, Florida, where we and the Rosenblums have homes.

Finally, my deepest gratitude goes to my wife, Chava, *a"h*, whose passing recently inspired me to share our life story for posterity.

Chapter I

My Childhood in Pre-War Poland

I N THE AFTERMATH of the great 1929 crash on Wall Street, I
came crying onto the world stage. I obviously knew nothing
about Wall Street until many years later. The only crash that I
did know then was, perhaps, of a toy that may have landed on the
floor. I was born on December 18, 1929 in Stopnica, a small town
of about 1500 inhabitants in south-central Poland, where my great
grandfather, Shaul Schwartz, was the *Rav*. *Rav* Schwartz was my
mother's grandfather. My parents, Avraham and Malka Wyszkowski
named me Yecheskel Menachem, or Chaskel for short. After a brief
stay in Otwock, where my grandfather, the famous *Rebbe* of Modzitz,
lived, we moved in with my father's parents. They lived some 14
miles away in Warsaw, the capital, at 5 Krasinski Square, across from
the Krasinski Gardens and the Supreme Court.

Today, Warsaw is a large metropolis with a population of 1.3 million. Much of the city was rebuilt after it had been destroyed along
with its Jewish population, of about 350,000, during World War II
and the Holocaust. Before the Holocaust, Warsaw was home to the
largest and the most thriving Jewish community in Europe. It was
the center of Torah learning and boasted many distinguished rabbis
and scholars, as well as flourishing Jewish businesses and industrial
concerns.[1]

---

1. Yitzchak Alfasi, *Jewish Glimpses of Warsaw* (New York: CIS, 1992).

Pre-war Krasinski Square.

Krasinski Square, 1936.

My mother, Malka Bina Taub.

My father, Avraham Wyszkowski.

My parents were married in 1928 in Kurtchev, a town with some 10,000 inhabitants in Otwock County, about half an hour by train from Warsaw. My mother was Malka Bina, daughter of the Modzitzer *Rebbe*, Shaul Yedidya Elozor, and Chava Taub, the second *Rebbetzin*. Her marriage to my father, Avraham, the son of Dovid Meyer, a wealthy soap manufacturer from Warsaw, and Sarah Wyszkowski, turned into a spectacular event. Unfortunately, my grandmother, Chava, had died from typhus several years earlier, and it was the third *Rebbetzin*, Nechama, who was present at the wedding. Thousands of *Chassidim* and non-*Chassidim* came by the trainload from Warsaw and other towns, arriving on the day of the wedding. Moreover, it was announced in advance that the *Rebbe* had invited the poor, who would be served first at special tables before the start of the wedding ceremony. As soon as word got out, thousands of poor people from all over Kurtchev and neighboring villages headed for the wedding. In addition, the non-Jewish dignitaries, including doctors and city officials of Otwock and Kurtchev, were entertained in a separate room.

The ceremony did not get under way until past midnight. The local police kept order in the flood-lit areas outside, where thousands had gathered. The following account of the wedding appeared in the Warsaw Jewish daily newspapers.[2] (Article written by Y. Borenstein.)

THE BIG WEDDING
BY THE MODZITZER REBBE KURTCHEV

7/6/1928

This past Tuesday, the Modzitzer *Rebbe, Harav* Shaul Taub, led his 18-year-old daughter, Malkale, to the *chuppah*. The *chosson*, Avraham, son of the wealthy Warsaw soap manufacturer Dovid Wyszkowski (Franciskaner St. 20), is also 18. He is considered a great *lamdan* and *yachsan*; his father is a *mechutan* of the Amshinover *Rebbe*.

This famous and sensational wedding took place in Kurtchev.

On *Motzoei Shabbos*, it was announced in the name of the *Rebbe*, that the next day, Sunday, a special meal with music would be held for the poor. Word of the feast rapidly spread throughout Kurtchev and the neighboring villages. Indeed, last Sunday, Kurtchev was flooded with the poor, both men and women, who made a pilgrimage to the *Rebbe's* festivity. The feast took place with great fanfare in the huge *Beis HaMedrash* – with rolls, fish, and whisky. The hungry poor, who were uplifted by this event, especially because of the presence of the *Rebbe*, sat at the long tables.

The *Rebbe*, with his powerful tenor voice, entertained the guests by singing his popular "Fifth Opera." The *Seuda* lasted some five hours. While they were having their feast, the *Rebbetzin* kept herself busy with the poor women. When their meal was finally over, she handed every poor man a Zloty for his trip back home.

A great number of *Chassidim* came to the wedding from Warsaw, Lodz, as well as many other towns. The Stopnitzer *Rov, Harav* Shaul Schwartz (the bride's grandfather from her mother's side), the Sobollover *Rebbe*, the Fallinitzer *Rov*, and others also honored the *chosson* and *kallah*.

At 4 o'clock, the *chosson* arrived on the *Koleike* (special train from Warsaw), in Kurtchev. He was greeted at the station by one hundred *Chassidim* on horseback, dressed as Cossacks and accompanied by two bands. The *chosson* was then led with great fanfare to the residence of R. Yitzchok Dozor. Soon the place was besieged by a large crowd of young and old, as well as many curious non-Jews from the town.

Meanwhile, the number of people in town grew by the hour, as

---

2. *Der Moment* (Warsaw), June 7, 1928, p. 4; *Unzer Express* (Warsaw), June 7, 1928, p. 2; Shimon Kanz, *Otwock-Korchev, Memorial Book* (Tel Aviv, 1968).

each Koleike brought in hundreds and hundreds more. To prevent chaos, the local police force, reinforced by volunteers from *Bikur Cholim* of Otwock, made special preparations for the occasion. Nevertheless, the situation just before the *chuppah*, indeed, became chaotic and most guests had to remain outside the huge *Beis Medrash*.

The *chuppah* finally got under way in the garden outside at 12 midnight, with the entire area being lit up with torch lights and lamps. Many people were on the nearby roofs and also hanging from the surrounding trees, to watch the ceremony.

By one o'clock in the morning, the *seuda* began, and continued until five in the morning. Tables were set in the *Beis HaMedrash*, in the women's section and outside in the garden. The famous *badchon*, R. Yisroel Weintraub, stood on a table and entertained the guests, while the orchestras of Skalmer and Buchnert played and presented "concerts."

Naturally, the Modzitze singers did not fall behind.

They sang operas and marches; in short the music played.

Then came the announcements of *droshe geshank* (wedding gifts), which took about an hour. The gifts, consisting of lots of silverware, came pouring in from both the *kallah's* and the *chosson's* side, although much more from the *kallah's* side.

Before *bentching*, the *Rebbe* presented a musical march which he repeated seven times. Everyone present easily learned the music and joined in the singing. After this was over, everyone joined in a dance to the tune of the *Rebbe's* march, which was accompanied by the orchestra.

According to the *Chassidim* and consistent with tradition, the real *simcha* begins with the reciting of the *Sheva Brochos*, when everyone joins in celebration.

In 1929, several months after the wedding, a devastating fire broke out and spread to some 18 houses in Kurtchev, including the *Rebbe's* house. Even before the firemen arrived, the townspeople had managed to pour many pails of water onto the fire. However, it was too late. The house in which they had lived for five years had to be abandoned.

Following this tragedy, and by popular demand of his *Chassidim*, the *Rebbe* moved to Otwock, a town with a population of some 43,000. Otwock then became the *Rebbe's* permanent residence. The *Rebbe's* arrival in town, where he first lived in rented quarters, stirred the *Chassidim* into action. They acquired a huge lot, upon which

די גרויסע חתונה ביים מאדזשיצער רבי'ן אין קאדטשעוו

The original newspaper article, written in Yiddish, describing the wedding of my parents, Avraham Wyszkowski to Malka Bina Taub, June 7, 1928.

גרויסע שריפה אין קאדטשעוו

The Fire in Kurtchev, 1929.

Modzitzer Yeshiva Tiferes Yisrael, Otwock.

Beis HaMedrash in Otwock.

they built a beautiful *Beis Medrash* (synagogue) and residential quarters for the *Rebbe* and his family. My parents decided to join them in Otwock, at least for a while. Together with my uncle Shlomo, my father's brother and son-in-law of the Amshinover *Rebbe*, they rented a nearby summer home.

Years later, in 1953, when I got married in Israel to my beloved wife Chava Besser, her mother, Devorah Leah, who came from Otwock, surprised me with the revelation that before the War, she had been friends with my parents in that town. Moreover, both my in-laws and my parents were married the same year.

Meanwhile, by 1931, my family moved in with my grandparents in Warsaw. In the years prior to the Nazi blitz on Poland in 1939, I attended the local *cheder* (*yeshiva*), where I learned Torah and took

some secular courses, like math
and Polish. With the exception of
the birth of my younger brother
Yisroel on June 24, 1934, that period in our lives was to me quite
uneventful. My dear mother,
soft-natured as she was, had attended to us and our daily needs
with love and affection.

My father took great pride in
having studied Talmud with the
renowned *Rav* Avraham Wein-
berg, from whom he gained a
commanding knowledge of rabbinic scholarship. Nevertheless,
he shunned all talk of pursuing
a rabbinic career and chose busi-

The Modzitzer *Rebbe*, Harav
Shaul Yedidya Elozor Taub, my
maternal grandfather.

ness instead, occasionally following his brother Moshe to the stock
exchange. My father had three brothers, Yehoshua, who died in
1906 at the age of three, Shlomo, who was later murdered with his
family by the Nazis, and Moshe, who escaped with his family during
the war and made it to the States. After my grandmother Sarah,
passed away in 1936, my very tall and dignified grandfather, Dovid
Meyer, a *talmid chochom* (Talmudic scholar), became somewhat withdrawn. Much of the time he chose to stay in his room and remained
non-communicative. However, he still found time to keep an eye
on his sons. My uncle Moshe was a very active businessman whose
attire was generally up-to-date. Whenever my uncle Moshe would
come to visit my grandfather, he would first stop in the lobby and
change his clothing. He would replace his modern hat with a black
hat with the front part bent up, before entering the house. During
the day, my grandfather would spend much of his time sitting with
a *Gemara* (a Talmudic volume) and studying. He would study at the
soap factory which he owned, on 24 *Franciszkanska* (Franciskaner)
Street, a very busy and bustling center. When a customer entered,
he would put away the book and attend to him. In a book on the
Amshinover *Rebbe*, *Rav* Yosef *zt"l*, whose daughter was married to

Harav Dovid Meyer Wyszkowski, my paternal grandfather. . .

my uncle Shlomo, the author, Yaakov Weisbrodt, describes my *Zeide*: "*Rav* Dovid Meyer Wyszkowski, who was among the old Amshinover *Chassidim*, engaged in Torah and charity. His mansion was well known as a place that was always open to guests and especially to the *rebbes* of Amshinov. He was a very wealthy man, and one of the most respected Jews in Warsaw."[3]

On *Shabbos*, my father and I would put on our *kapotes* (a long black garment), go to *Shul* (synagogue) to pray and then return home to eat the *Shabbos* meal. After we settled in Warsaw, my father would take me from time to time for *Shabbos* and Yom Tov (the Jewish Holidays) to Otwock, to be with the *Rebbe* and get a good spot at his *Tish* (a festive meal) in the big *Beis HaMedrash*. Although many *Rebbes*

3. Haynt, *Sept. 18, 1929, p. 6*; יעקב ד. ויסברוד, אהל יוסף: בית אמשינאוו, (תל אביב: תשע"ד), דף תמ"ז.

Sarah Wyszkowski, my paternal grandmother.

lived in Otwock, the most popular *Rebbe* by far, was Modzitz. On any given day hundreds of people headed for Modzitz, and on holidays, thousands would come.

Each visit to the *Rebbe* was a memorable one, not easily forgotten. Especially memorable were the beautiful new *nigunim* (melodies), which he composed every year. Everyone's spirit was uplifted and inspired by his powerful tenor voice and harmonious, soul-stirring

Yisroel, 5 years old, 1939.   Chaskel, 10 years old, 1939.

"operas" and marches. This was especially inspiring on Rosh Hashana and Yom Kippur when thousands crowded into the *Beis HaMedrash* and many others on the street outside. Indeed, seeing the huge mass of people, standing pressed together, was an amazing, impressive, and unforgettable sight. Everyone was riveted in his place for hours, eagerly swallowing every syllable and sound that emanated from the saintly voice of the *Rebbe*.

As for the summer, my entire family, like many other families, would usually spend time in the cool and pleasant atmosphere of Otwock.[4] It was Otwock where the first German bombs fell and World War II began.

Many things in life today that are taken for granted, such as radios, fans in the summer, and telephones, were for us and for most people in Poland rare and not readily available. My grandfather's factory was the exception. He had not only one telephone but two.

During those pre-war years, there were occasional attacks on Jews by street gangs, mostly the Endeks. In one such attack, my father was struck and came home with a bloody nose. On Christian holi-

---

4. *Chaskel Wyszkowski*, The Modzitzer Rebbe *(New York, 2010), pp. 8–10.*

WARSZAWA   Ul. Frańciszkańska

Franciszkanska (Franciskaner) Street in pre-war Warsaw.

days we would avoid being out in the street, where a Jew could be mugged, especially during a Christian parade where the marchers carried various church symbols. Otherwise, everything seemed to me, as a young boy, (I was only 10 when the war broke out in 1939) quite normal.

That was not the situation of the Jewish community as a whole. Polish independence, in 1918, was inaugurated with anti-Jewish outbreaks and violence by the Polish army. At that time, the one country in the world where Jewish activity took on the widest dimension was Poland. At the time there were 3.5 million Jews, the largest concentration of Jews in Europe. By the 1922 elections, Jews won 34 out of 444 seats in the Sejm (parliament). In order to prevent the government's attempts to deprive minority representatives of their rights, which were guaranteed for the newly born Polish Republic in June 28, 1919, in the League of Nations Minorities Treaty, the Jewish faction joined other minorities as a block in the Sejm. Of the total population, 10% were Jews, but 30% were concentrated in the big cities.

Whereas non-Jews were mostly employed in agriculture, Jews, at first, dominated business and manufacturing.[5] In the eyes of the Polish government, the Jews were viewed as a disruptive element along with the nationalist communists, whom the government sought to destroy, or at least to suppress. After several deceitful attempts, and while pretending to honor its commitments to the League of Nations to protect free speech and equality of the Jews, the government finally succeeded in breaking up the minority bloc and Jewish power. With the impending economic difficulties, the government attempted to blame the Jews for all their problems.

Be this as it may, the economic, political and social pressure upon the Jews in the late 1920s was unable to save Poland from devaluation, which was the result of German inflation. Additionally, it could not prevent the depression and unemployment that followed in the 1930s. Every crisis triggered more attacks against the power of the Jews; in short, Russian tyranny was replaced by Polish tyranny.[6] The impoverishment of the Jewish artisan and small trader was a deliberate and continuous process and by 1935, the Jewish situation had seriously deteriorated. Encouraged by Nazi propaganda heard over radio Berlin and inspired by nationalistic fervor, anti-Semitism and the Catholic Church, the Polish government launched a more brazen assault against the Jewish community. In 1936, it virtually banned kosher *shechita* (slaughtering) and introduced an unofficial *numerus clausus* – a quota system limiting the number of Jews in universities.

In 1938, under the new dictator Rydz Szmigly, the already reduced Jewish student population was assigned separate benches on the left side of the lecture halls (to identify them with the leftist and communist movements). In reaction, Jewish students chose to stand throughout their classes rather than sit on those benches. Moreover, fascist gangs, the most notorious among them, the Endeks and the

5. Raphael Mahler, *The Jews in Poland Between Two World Wars* (in Hebrew) (Tel Aviv: Dvir, 1968), pp. 35–7.

6. Ismar Elbogen, *A Century of Jewish Life* (Philadelphia: JPS, 1966), pp. 532–33; A. Malamat, *A History of the Jewish People* (Cambridge, MA: Harvard University Press, 1976), pp. 957–60; Paul Mendes-Flohr and Yehuda Reinharz, eds., *The Jew in the Modern World, A Documentary History* (New York: Oxford University Press, 1995), pp. 437–39.

די הינטערקוליסען פון שטאדט-ראט
בעשלוס וועגען דער שחיטה

דער דאנערשטאגדיגער בעשלוס פון
שטאדטראט וועגען דער אידישער
שחיטה, וועלכער פיהרט איין פאקטיש
א בענרעניצונג פון דער שחיטה האט
פריהער אויסגערופען נאך א גרעסערע
ווי ער אא פארטעשטעלט געווארען.
מאדרן פלעגט אין דער זיצונג און עם
איז נעקומען צו סקאנדאלען מיט די
אידישער ראטסמענער. דער סטאגראל
האט נעהאט פאלנענדען מערלויף.

זיין רעפעראט רעזומירט די מיינונגען
פון דער קאמיסיע אין דעם זין. דאם
מען ראמ'ף באלד בערעצען די די אידישע
שחיטה אויף 33 פראצענט אן נעברעג
מאבען אנ'אקמ'מע כיי אלע אידישע
איינוואוינער. צי זיי עטען רוזוא כשר
פלייש און ווימיעל פראצענט אידען
עם טוען נישט קיין כשר בלייז עוו.

פינע זוויינער, א שעה מאר דער זי
צונג פון שטאדטראט האט דער ווינע
שטאדטר-פרעזידענט ה' אלפינסקי גע
רומען די זיצונג פון דער אפראויזיאיע
קאמיסיע וועגען פאראייניכטומליכען דעם
רעפעראט וועגען דער שחיטה-פראנע.
עס האט זיך ארויסגעווידען, אז דער
רעמעראטנט פולק, לעזאואנדראוסקי האט
נישט נעקאנט רעטעירען זיין שטאארט
ראם צוליב דעם לעניאנען - צוזאמענ
פאהר אין דעם רעפעראט האט איבער
נענומען ארוו. מיערושאנקאוסקי.
ארוו. מיערושאנקאוסקי האט אין

זיין רעפעראם רעזומירט די מיינונגען
פון דער קאמיסיע אין דעם זין, דאם
מען ראמ'ף באלד בערעצען די אידישע
שחיטה אויף 33 פראצענט און נעברעג
מאבען אנ'אקמ'מע כיי אלע אידישע
אינוואוינער, צי זיי עטען רוזוא כשר
פלייש און ווימיעל פראצענט אידען
עם טוען נישט קיין כשר בלייז עוו
פיעל פראצענטס וועם מען אברעכענען
פון די דערמאהנטע 33 פראצענט.

די דאזיגע אויספיהרונגען האבען
ארויסנערופען א שטורמישען פראטעסט
פון דער זייט פון די אידישע ראטסמר
נער. וועלכע האבען אנגעוויזען, אז ארוו.
מיערושאנקאוסקי האם שלעכט דער
מעירם די מיינונגען פון דער קאמיסיע.
און זיי קאמיסיע פון דער קאמיסיע
בעשלוסען נישט אננענומען. די אידען
האבען ערקלערם. אז זיי וועלמען פאר
רען, דאם די נאנצע שחיטה - פראנע
זאל אווענעשטעלט ווערען אין דער
נאצצער ברייט אויפ'ן פלענום און דער
פלענום וועט אליין אורמיילען וועגען

דער פראנע.
אויך דער ענדעקישער ראטסמאן קרוו-
זע האט אויסגעדריקט זיין אונצומירעני-
היים מיט דעם מארשלאו פון 33 פרא-
צענט און ערקלערם, אז ער וועם שטרע-
רען צו פערבאסמען אינגאנצען די אר-
דישע שחיטה.

פרעו. אלפינסקי האט ערקלערם. אז
הגם אויף די בעראטוגגען פון דער קא-
מיסיע איז קיין בעשלום וועגען פערקלע-
נערען די שחיטה נישט אנגעוומען גע-
וואהען. דאך איז צו רערינגען פון די רע
דעם. אז מען דארף שטרעבען צו פער-
קלענערען דאם שעבטען לויט'ן אורי-
שען רין.

נאך 2 שעה רייסמני'שען איז מען
ווי עם איז דורבנעטקומען און נעאיינינט
זיך אויף דער בעסקסמער פאראוצילע
וועלכע ערקלערם. אז זיי וועלכע פאר
נרעצענען דאם אידישע שחיטה אלם עקא
נאמישע נויטווענדינקיים.

Haynt, Dec. 23 1935.

Naras, roamed in uniform through the streets of Poland, indiscriminately attacking Jews, provoking disturbances as well as desecrating synagogues and cemeteries. On the eve of the Nazi invasion of 1939, with over a million unemployed, the Jews of Poland were demoralized, living every moment with the fear of possible expulsion or starvation. While they waited, Hitler was making preparations for the invasion of Poland.[7]

7. Louis Finkelstein, ed., *The Jews* (New York: Schocken, 1970), pp. 380–82; Howard M. Sachar, *The Course of Modern Jewish History* (New York: Vintage Books, 1990), pp. 424–30.

Chapter II

Escape to Vilna

O N September 1, 1939, at 6:30 A.M., Germany launched the invasion. Minutes later on that Friday morning, while still standing in prayer in my grandfather's *Beis Medrash* in Otwock, we heard the sounds of approaching planes flying high in the sky. As we rushed to the windows, the sound of heavy blasts was suddenly heard coming from a short distance away. The Germans hit a Jewish orphanage, killing eight young children, and the Sch-weitzer Villa, where 15 more people were killed. These were the first Jewish victims of the war.[1]

Although we didn't know what to expect and there was much confusion, some immediate steps were taken. We began to dig ditches out in the yard and remove all of the *Rebbe*'s *seforim* from the shelves, and hid them down in the cellar. In the meantime, a unit of Polish cavalry stationed its horses in our yard. The horses, apparently starving, soon began to chew the wooden fence.

My father, who was then only 29 years old, was ready for action. He insisted that the *Rebbe* and the men in the family leave at once for Vilna, a city in northeastern Poland far away from the German front. Moreover, aside from the Nazi invasion, because of their age, he and some of my uncles also had to fear the possibility of being drafted into the Polish army. After initial resistance to my father's demand

---

1. Finkelstein, *The Jews*, pp. 388–89.

Jewish Orphanage after
bombing, Otwock, 1939.
(*Courtesy of Yad Vashem*)

and threat to go it alone, the *Rebbe*, my father and two of my uncles,
Chaskel and Yitzhok, left for Vilna in a hurry on a truck that had
already been loaded to capacity with people trying to escape. The
women and children (myself included) were to follow later. Thanks
to my father's insistence, most of us survived the war.

The British Jewish historian Martin Gilbert, a Fellow of Merton
College in Oxford, England, put the situation in the right perspec-
tive:

> For six and a half years, Poland's Jews had watched with alarm
> the violent anti-Semitism imposed by Nazi Germany, first upon
> German, then upon Austrian, and finally upon Czech Jewry.
> They knew, at first hand, from Polish anti-Semites, what mob
> hatred could do. But Polish Jewry had its own means of defense,
> its own press, its own institutions, and its own representation in
> the Polish parliament. With the German invasion, these protec-
> tive shields were torn away. On the railway carriages bringing
> German troops into the war zone, were painted crude pictures
> of Jews with hooked noses, and the slogan: "We're off to Poland
> – to thrash the Jews."[2]

2. Martin Gilbert, *The Holocaust* (New York: Holt, Reinhart and Winston, 1985), p. 84.
See also Nora Levin, *The Holocaust* (New York: Crowell, 1978).

A Villa in Otwock after the German Attack, 1939.

In Hitler's mind, as we now know, war and annihilation of the Jews were interdependent. In less than a month, once the Luftwaffe had gained control of the skies of Poland, the German army swept across the western part while the Russians seized the east. With the fall of Warsaw on September 27, 1939, hostilities in Poland came to an end. Partition, based on the secret Russo-German pact of August 23, and not a new idea in this country's history, was established once again. In those early days of the war, few Polish Jews and not many Russians, for that matter, knew what was really at stake, nor how Hitler and his gangsters were plotting against them.

Although it was possible to travel in the first few weeks after the Polish surrender, we stayed put in Otwock together with the rest of the *Rebbe*'s family, and rarely ventured out. My mother and I did go to Warsaw for one day, only to find nothing but a hollow shell that had once been the large apartment house in which we had lived. Except for German soldiers or units of the infamous Gestapo, the streets of Warsaw were largely abandoned.

Shortly after the city fell, several members of the Gestapo entered my grandfather's soap factory, emptied it, tortured him by ripping out his long beard and then shot to death my uncle Shlomo, my

October, 1939.

1946. Nazis and Poles Cutting beards of Jews.

father's brother, who was also at the plant. My grandfather, had suffered critical wounds from which he never recovered. On November 25, 1939 he succumbed to his injuries and died from a heart attack. Thus they became the first victims, *HY"D*, in our family.

The Germans rounded up Jews caught in the streets, abused and humiliated them by cutting off half their beards with a knife, and even tearing it out. They also forced other indignities upon them.[3] Therefore, we quickly returned to Otwock, where we felt safer.

---

3. Gilbert, *The Holocaust*, pp. 90–2.

Krasinski Square, 1945.

One day during the first week of German occupation, several members of the Gestapo raided the *Rebbe's* home in Otwock. They looked around the large room in which we were all gathered. Then suddenly one of them turned to me, as I was standing at the door, and demanded to know why I was there. "I don't live here," came my reply (thinking this would be the safest answer). "Rous!"(Get out) he screamed, accompanied by a slap on my cheek, so I made a quick exit. As I bolted out, I saw the largest *Shul* in Otwock going up in flames, with no fire trucks in sight.

Early in January 1940, a Polish guide, sent by the *Rebbe* to get us out, finally arrived from Vilna. So, our family got itself organized and prepared to leave. My mother, *a"h*, chose to stay behind with my younger brother Yisroel, until my grandfather Wyszkowski's estate was settled, a decision that tragically sealed her and my brother's fate. Unfortunately, this was the last time I saw her and my brother.

Remains of our residence after German bombing, Krasinski Square, 1945.

Their fate, which could have also been my own, although uncertain to this day, was most probably the horror of most Warsaw Ghetto Jews – the Treblinka gas chambers.

We left by train the next day and headed for the German-Russian border in the east. After a short ride, we arrived in Malkinia, only five miles north of Treblinka, where the Nazis later opened the infamous death camp. Our group consisted of the Polish guide, *Rebbetzin* Brocho Esther (the *Rebbe's* wife), Hershel – her three-year-old son, my young uncles – Yisroel, 13 and Dovid, 10, myself, 10, and Shmuel Finkelstein, a close friend of the family. At the time, the absence of my mother and brother did not worry me too much, since I assumed (wrongly) that they would soon join us. But, the responsibilities of this flight soon convinced us that, overnight, we had all become adults. Finkelstein and my Uncle Yisroel helped the Polish guide keep us on the right track as we struggled across the border area.

There were two gates at the station; one for Poles and the other for Jews. The Germans at the gate confiscated the *Rebbetzin's* fur coat and all her jewelry, but missed the one hundred dollar bills that my mother had secretly hidden in my shirt. As we were heading to no-man's land between the borders, the temperature outside was about 40 degrees below zero centigrade. After a short walk in the dark, we reached a place where thousands of refugees were squatting around bonfires for warmth. They were mostly Jews trying to escape from the Nazis and cross over to the Russian side of the border.

Since the Polish guide was anxious to attempt a night crossing, after only a brief rest, we followed him silently in the snow and sub-freezing temperature into a forest on the border. Suddenly, three Russian soldiers with fixed bayonets appeared as if from nowhere, and without a word we retreated back to no-man's land. The attempt had failed.

The next morning, we again set out and headed straight for the border. As we were moving between the heavy trees through the forest, we suddenly caught sight of a Russian military detachment, crossing the field beyond the forest. Afraid of being discovered, we hid standing silently behind the trees, while the *Rebbetzin* tried to keep a glove over Hershel's mouth to keep him from crying. This time we made it. Now that the forest was safely behind us, we moved quickly toward the first house in the open field, where transportation in the form of a sled had been pre-arranged for us by the guide. As we entered the house, we found the Polish peasant and his wife sitting on the oven eating directly from a big pot of cabbage.

The next few days were quite uneventful. All six of us – the *Rebbetzin*, Hershel (her son), my uncles Yisroel and Dovid, Finkelstein and I –were packed onto the sled with several blankets for protection from the icy weather. We headed for the Russian-Lithuanian border, with just two stops in Bialystok and in Reishe. Vilna, our final stop, had been seized by the Russians at the outbreak of the war, during their sweep of eastern Poland. It was ostensibly returned to the Lithuanians, who claimed it as their historic capital. Later, by June 15, 1940, the Russians would again seize Vilna along with the entire Lithuania. Although our journey across the border occurred without incident, we were one of the last to be so fortunate. Once the Polish guide bribed the Lithuanian guards, we were on our way. By mid-January, we finally reached Vilna, the Jerusalem of Lithuania, where I joined my father, the *Rebbe*, my uncles and aunts.

My father and I stayed in Vilna for over a year until February, 1941. Harav Chaim Ozer Grodzenski, *zt"l*, the world renowned rabbinical sage and towering *posek* of Vilna, was gracious enough to

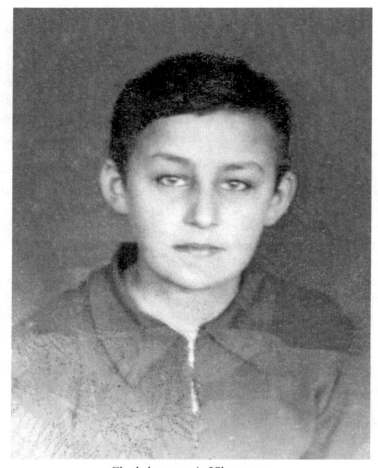

Chaskel, age 11, in Vilna, 1940.

make his residence the temporary address of the *Zeide*, the *Rebbe*. Moreover, he dispatched urgent letters and cables (see below) to the rabbinical organizations and the *Vaad Hatzalah* (Rescue Committee) in the United States, calling for their immediate aid.

Vilna became the hub for tens of thousands of Jewish refugees from all over Poland, among them many distinguished *Rebbes*, *Roshei Yeshivas*, who in some cases escaped with their *yeshivas*, and also scores of scholars and community leaders.[4] Numerous *yeshivas* such

---

4. Edward Phillips, ed., *Flight and Rescue* (Washington D.C., 2001), pp. 14–17.

Harav Chaim Ozer Grodzenski.

The Amshinover *Rebbe*,
Harav Shimon Kalish.

as those of Mir, consisting of some 300 young men, Kletzk, Radin, Kamenitz, Baranovich, and Bialystok arrived nearly intact. In addition there were also some men from the *yeshivas* of Grodno, Volozhin, Lomza, Lutzk, Beis Yosef, Lublin, Lubavitch, Slonim, and Mezritch. Moreover, famous *rebbes*, including my *Zeide*, the Modzitzer, and the Amshinover, found refuge in Vilna. The Amshinover *Rebbe*, *Rav* Shimonle, who also came from Otwock, was followed by thousands of refugees who had great faith in him and his advice. Many of those refugees, including the Mirrer Yeshiva, later joined him in Kobe, Japan and later in Shanghai, China. *Rav* Shimonle's niece was the wife of Shlomo, *HY"D*, my father's brother.

The majestic appearance, in Vilna and Kovno, of the Modzitzer *Rebbe*, one of the most popular Chassidic *rebbes* in Poland, was indeed a singular event in this heartland of the *Misnagdim* (those opposed to *Chassidim*). His conduct of the *Shabbos tish* and *Shalosh Seudos*, took the Jewish community by storm. Thousands of refugees, *Chassidim* and *Misnagdim* alike, converged to hear the *Rebbe* and were uplifted from their distress by his Torah and *neginah*. Altogether over 20,000 refugees managed to escape to Vilna.[5]

Although the news that reached us from Warsaw and Otwock was very discouraging, we hoped that my mother and younger brother

---

5. Wyszkowski, *The Modzitzer Rebbe*, pp. 25–6.

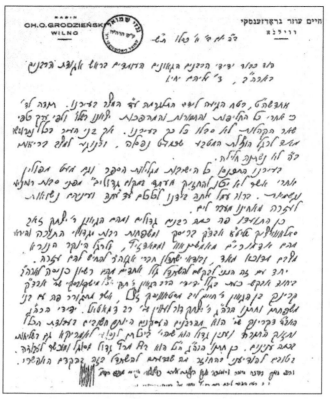

Letter from Harav Grodzenski, 1940.

would eventually somehow find their way to us. Unfortunately, by October 1940, all Jews living in Warsaw and the neighboring towns, including Otwock, were forced into the newly created Warsaw Ghetto, from which escape was virtually impossible.[6]

Meanwhile, although letters were exchanged between my father and mother, there were long delays and these exchanges were sporadic. At times she would not get letters for several weeks and then, suddenly, three or four would arrive on the same day. This was caused, apparently, and perhaps deliberately, by Nazi censorship. Indeed, my mother, who was certainly not fully aware of the

6. Raul Hilberg, *The Destruction of the European Jews* (New York: Quadrangle Books, 1973), p. 148.

Chaskel (right) with uncle Dovid and friends in Vilna, 1940.

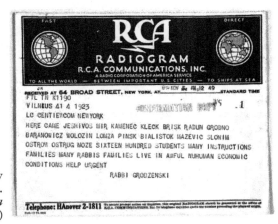

Cable from Harav
Grodzenski, 1940.
(*Courtesy of Yeshiva
University Archives*)

real circumstances, complained bitterly, suspecting and blaming my
father for these delays. She charged him with a lack of concern and
with being insensitive to her plight. The following is a letter from
my mother to my father in Vilna dated January 27, 1940:

Dear Abraham:
What are you doing? How is your health? How is Chaskush
[that's me] and daddy [the *Rebbe*] and everybody else? I wrote
you a few letters and didn't get any response. I am still writing
you. If you have any compassion for me, then please write me at
least a few words . . .

Again in still another letter sent a few days later, she writes:

Dear Abraham:
What happened? Why are you not writing? Write me right away.
What should I do, and will we ever see each other? It seems to
me that you forgot that I even exist. Please write me whether I
should buy (anything) for you and if you received everything for
Chaskush . . .

In a letter dated March 7, 1940 to the *Rebbe* – my grandfather – even
before being forced into the Warsaw Ghetto, my mother warned
him that "if I stay longer I will have no more food, and I am going to
die here, together with my child, of starvation. Since I am left here
with my child, I plead that you do whatever you can. Please, do not
forget me."[7]

A year later, on April 12, 1941, by which time my *zeide*, the *Rebbe*,
had already arrived in New York, he sent postcards in German to
my mother and her sister Feigel in the Warsaw Ghetto, both of
which were returned by the German censor. However, my father did
remain in contact until as late as July 28, 1941, in Kobe, Japan, at
which time he received the last postcard from my mother.

All except the first of my mother's 30 letters were written in
Polish, not in Yiddish which was the language we spoke at home.
Yiddish was most likely banned by the Germans, perhaps to accommodate their censors. As for my father, he sent food to my mother
in addition to the regular letters. He would empty large aluminum
containers of pickles and fill them with fat, an item which, under the
starving conditions in the Ghetto, was desperately needed. Never-

---

7. Correspondence between my father and mother, 1939–41.

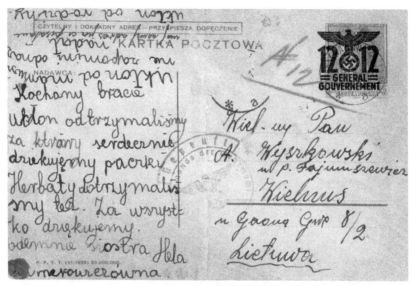

Postcard from my mother, Vilna, 1940.

theless, from my mother's letters it is clear that she had very little money and was often forced to sell some of her and my brother's clothes to survive. Once they were forced into the Ghetto, living conditions were horrible. On the average, there were as many as six to a room.

My mother and brother, Malka Bina and Yisroel Wyszkowski, *H"yd*, Warsaw Ghetto, *1940*.

Meanwhile, in Vilna, my father registered me in a local *yeshiva* where I was able to continue my studies. Severe lack of money made daily living a hardship for my father and the rest of the family while making any future travel plans nearly impossible.

When my father, my uncles and the *Rebbe* escaped from Otwock, they had merely taken some clothes with them, most of which were stolen on the way by Polish peasants. In a Hebrew letter to Yaakov Kapelusznik (Cappell), the *Rebbe's* wealthy brother-in-law in Belgium, dated January 17, 1940, my father writes:

My mother Malka Bina with her sister, Feigel, *H"yd, 1927.*

Dear Uncle:

I am very surprised that the money that you sent us has not yet arrived, although the sweaters did. It is possible that it was confiscated by the authorities, since it is forbidden by law to receive foreign currency by mail. I pray that G-d will have mercy, because at this time and without exaggeration, every bit of money helps keep 12 souls alive. We have no one here to help us. Please, once again, have pity and help us in our dilemma. . . .[8]

Moreover, hundreds of dollars were also needed for each individual to provide for any eventual travel plans.

Aside from that, my *Zeide,* the *Rebbe,* was confronted with another problem. He was worried that due to his distress and concern for family members under the Nazis he might forget hundreds of *nigunim* (songs), the epitome of his fame, which he had composed during the pre-war years. He therefore engaged a composer who was able to record the melodies as the *Rebbe* sang before him, thereby preserving most of his musical compositions. These notes were redone and given a final polish after he came to the States. Indeed, a great treasure was saved. Years later in the United States, the *Zeide* once said at his *tish* (*Shabbos* meal) that he keeps all his worries in a suitcase, which he opens each day for only an hour, to meditate over them.

During his stay in Vilna, the *Rebbe* prayed and held a *tish* at the *Beis Medrash* of the *Chassidim* of Keidinov, where hundreds would gather to listen eagerly to his Torah and *neginah*. On Pesach, we gathered for the *seder* in the *Zeide's* residence and celebrated until early dawn. Many *Chassidim* and *Misnagdim* waited outside making vain attempts, during the night, to push open the door. The *Rebbe* insisted that our *seder* remain a family celebration. Although traditionally the *seder* is an occasion for joy, everyone at the table was fully aware of the absence and suffering of my brother and mother, her sisters, Golda and Feigel, as well as their husbands and children.

Unfortunately, my mother Malka, *a"h,* and brother Yisroel, *a"h,* died *al Kiddush Hashem* along with many family members; my moth-

---

8. Yaakob Cappell, Israel Cappell ed. אמת ליעקב (B'nei B'rak, Israel), p. 223.

Thousands of Warsaw Jews Escaping toward Vilna, 1939.
(Courtesy of YIVO Archives)

er's sister Feigel, and husband *Rav* Yechiel Danziger, as well as their children, Chava-Sara and Shmuel-Tzvi, my father's brother Shlomo Wyszkowski, his wife Tzipora and their children, and my mother's brother-in-law, *Rav* Chaim-Yosef Finkler. The only ones to survive were my mother's sister, Golda Finkler, and her daughter, Kaya.

Chapter III

Russian Dilemma – Welcome to Japan

A s THE OMINOUS REPORTS from Warsaw, Lodz, Krakow, and other places in Poland began to arrive almost daily, it became very clear to most people in Vilna that preparations must be made to leave the city before it was too late. Attempts to that end were made by the *Zeide*, who asked his son *Rav* Shmuel-Eliyahu Taub, in Tel Aviv, to try and obtain certificates for the entire family for travel to *Eretz* Yisrael. When my *Zeide* was *niftar* in December 1947, *Rav* Shmuel succeeded him as the Modzitzer *Rebbe*. My *Zeide* also communicated with *Rav* Yitzchok, his brother in New York, requesting an affidavit for the family, without which it would be impossible to obtain a visa to the United States.[1] At first these two destinations, Palestine and America, seemed to be the only available options. By February 1940, certificates from Tel Aviv and an affidavit from New York, for the *Rebbe* and some of his family, finally arrived.[2]

Unfortunately, the problems had only just begun. In the first place, money was not available to cover the heavy travel expenses, no matter which option would be used. Besides, even with the certificates, passage to Palestine was being hampered by the British. As for the alternative, prospects for immigration to the United States were generally quite bleak, since they were based on a very limited

---

1. Cappell, אמת, p. 222.

2. Cappell, אמת, pp. 222, 224.

quota system – the Immigration Act of 1924. In 1940, for instance, the Polish quota at first offered a two-year wait for only 6,524 visas.[3] Besides, even the *Zeide* and family had a long way to go before they could get a visa. But pressure from many Jewish and non-Jewish organizations, moved the State Department to make some minimal non-quota exceptions for the refugees. Of the 2,178 Polish Jews who went through Japan in 1940–1941, only 532 were eventually permitted to enter the United States. The *Rebbe* had bitterly complained in a letter to his Belgian brother-in-law about the American consul in Kovno, Lithuania, Bernard Gufler, as being "obnoxious, tough, and very demanding."[4]

For most of the refugees, the first and most immediate goal was to get out of Russia. The nearest place of refuge was Japan. During 1940, the window of opportunity for non-quota emergency visas to the United States was indeed very small. Two consular officials, Jan Zwartendijk, the Dutch consul, and Chiune Sugihara, the Japanese consul, appeared on the scene at the right moment.

Jewish refugees had to get from Vilna to Japan as quickly as possible and could not wait for an American visa to be granted. But in order to do that a destination beyond Japan was necessary, because the Japanese would only grant a transit visa.

With the help of the Dutch consul, the Caribbean island of Curacao, for which a visa was not really required, suddenly came up as a destination. When the Dutch ambassador in Latvia was asked by his Consul in Kovno whether to issue visas to Curacao, he replied: "No visa to Curacao was required, only a landing permit." In view of the urgency of the situation he was then asked to stamp into the passports only the first part, "No visa to Curacao required" to which he readily agreed. David Kranzler refers to it as a "legal fiction" and indeed some would-be immigrants did not believe this to be real. Thereupon the Dutch consul, Jan Zwartendijk, followed the ambassador's instructions, and handed out these so-called "Curacao visas," which he himself wrote and signed. Many refugees took the train to

---

3. Phillips, *Flight and Rescue*, p. 58.

4. Cappell, אמת p. 225.

Chiune Sugihara, 1940.   Jan Zwartendijk, 1940.

Kovno to obtain this piece of paper without any confidence that it would get them anywhere.

Nevertheless, they hoped that based on the Curacao paper, the Japanese would issue a transit visa, and the Russians an exit permit. Sugihara, the first ever Japanese consul to Lithuania, had arrived at his post in November, 1939. His real mission, assigned to him by the Japanese ambassador in Berlin, was to gather intelligence on German troop movements. He frequently went to border areas to monitor activities, camouflaging these trips as family picnics.[5]

One morning in late July, 1940, Sugihara awoke to an unusual noise outside the consulate. "There were people outside and they were talking very loudly. I went to the window of my apartment and looked out to see what was going on. I saw a crowd of Polish refugees behind the fences. . . . Each day the crowd grew bigger." They

---

5. Ron Greene, *Visas for Freedom: The Remarkable Story of Chiune and Yukika Sugihara* (Kovno: Sugihara Family Foundation, 1995–96); David Kranzler, *The Japanese, Nazis and Jews* (Hoboken: Ktav, 1988), pp. 310–12. See also part of the Sugihara's Transit Visa list, including my father's name, (my name as a minor is not mentioned separately) in Appendix.

Refugees in front of the
Japanese consulate in
Kovno, 1940.

pleaded for Japanese transit visas to leave Russia. Thereupon Sugihara sought advice from his Foreign Office, but did not get an immediate response. He therefore decided, in view of the desperation
of the refugees, and ignoring the possibility of rejection by Tokyo,
to issue the visas immediately, regardless of whether the recipients
were able to produce the necessary documents.[6]

During August 1940, visas were given by the hundreds each day
to the waiting refugees. Sugihara pressed ahead with the visas until
the end of the month, when he was ordered by the Soviet authorities, who had by then returned to Lithuania, to close his legation
in Kovno. Even after he boarded the train for his reassignment in
Berlin, he continued to stamp visas and hand them out first at the
station and then even through the window of the train. Despite op-
position in Tokyo to his extravagance in helping the refugees, the
total number of visas issued was well over 2,000.

On June 14, 1940, Russian troops swept back into Lithuania, Latvia, and Estonia. Tanks came rolling through the streets of Vilna and
all the other cities. By July 14, the three states had been incorporated
into the Soviet Republic.

To cross and leave the Soviet Union, for whatever destination,
one needed an exit visa – a very tough proposition. The refugees
were viewed by the Russian authorities as "refugee traitors." Marvin
Tokayer offers the following description of the dangers faced in ap-
plying for an exit permit from the Russians:

> "One by one they would be called into the NKVD (Soviet secret
> police). . . . Sitting in a bare cell of an office, pinned down by the

---

6. Phillips, *Flight and Rescue*, pp. 65–6.

NN.	NATIONALITY	NAME	ENTRANCE OR TRANSIT	DATE OF VISA	SASHOOBIO	BIKOO
379	POLNISCH	Jakob... SAPIR	"	30/VII	2	
380	"	Boruch PIEKARZ	"	"	2	
381	"	Alekeander ROZENHOLC	"	"	2	
382	"	Regina SPEISER	"	"	2	
383	"	JOZEF NUSBAUM	"	"	2	
384	"	Hanna OBERTYNSKA	"	"	2	
385	"	Leon STERNBERG	"	"	2	
386	"	Tola SAPIR	"	"	2	
387	"	Irena HALPERN	"	"	2	·
388	"	Jerzy-Jan HALpern	"	"	2	
389	"	Maria-JaninaKUBICKA	"	"	2	
390	"	Lubwicz KUBICKI	"	"	2	
391	"	Zofia KUBICKA	"	"	2	
392	"	Mojsiej LANDMAN	"	"	2	
393	"	Ber MIEDNECKI	"	"	2	
394	"	Ajchenblat EMANUEL	"	"	2	
395	"	Mordcha SIEMIATYCZ	"	"	2	
396	"	Hinda SIEMIATYCZ	"	"	2	
397	"	Kohn Majer Szulin	"	"	2	
398	"	Srol-Ejna ZARACHOWICZ	"	"	2	
399	"	Aria WILNER	"	"	2	
400	"	Wilner Regina	"	"	2	
401	"	Jozef BACH	"	"	2	
402	"	Benjamin SADOWSKI	"	"d	2	
403	"	Rubin Zylberman	"	"	2	
404	"	Elka Eichenblatt	"	"	2	
405	"	Lipa ZILBERMAN	"	"	2	
406	"	Szmul KAPTAN	"	"	2	
407	"	Frydchaj Hersz MENA- CHEM	"	"	2	
408	"	Trokenheim Hirsz Zelig	"	"	2	
409	"	Jankiel TROKENHEIM	"	"	2	
410	"	Izydor-Iszael NEUGOLIBERG	"	"	2	
411	"	Gutgeld Wolf	"	"	2	
412	"	Artur Marceli Goteman	"	"	2	
413	"	Abram WYSZKOWSKI	"	"	2	
414	"	Jerzy KAPLAN	"	"	2	
415	"	Garden Boruch Gert	"	"	2	
416	"	Aleksander WILNIER	"	"	2	
417	"	Naten-Majer OUTGELI	"	"	2	
418	"	LEWI GUTGELD	"	"	2	

Sugihara's Original List, 1939. My father's name appears as number 413.

cold piercing stare of a hostile interrogator, a would-be emigrant had to cope with a hundred questions, even the most innocent of which could be a death trap. . . . Then the interview was finished and you left. Whether you passed or failed, you had no idea. That you would learn from Intourist (a Russian travel agency). And Intourist continued to say nothing."[7]

When the *Rebbe's* turn came to enter the NKVD office for an exit permit, he appeared in his *Shabbos* clothes and declared that our Torah fully supports their Socialist ideas. It insists that a worker be

---

7. Wyszkowski, *The Modzitzer Rebbe*, pp. 27; Marvin Tokayer, *The Fugu Plan* (New York: Weatherhill, 1979), p. 96.

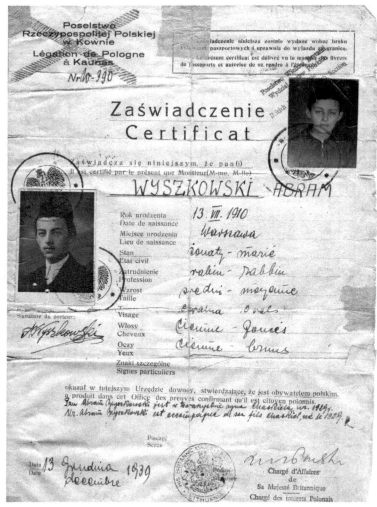

Front page of our visa documents, 1940.

treated with dignity and be paid on time. He assured the Russian agents, that if granted an exit, he would, upon arrival in the United States, make public the great Socialist ideas of the Soviet Union. The agents were apparently so impressed by his imposing figure and his convincing arguments that the *Rebbe* was the first to obtain the permit. Moreover, thanks to the *Rebbe*, many others were now also fortunate in getting the permit, including the Mirrer Yeshiva, and

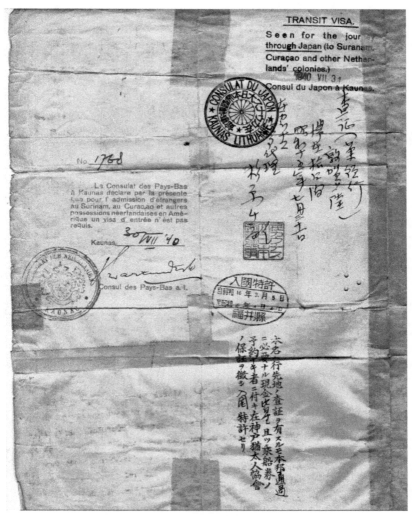

Our Japanese transit visa and Curacao visa, 1940.

other *Rebbes*. In fact, when the *Rebbe* arrived in New York, he called for a press conference, at which he kept his word and praised the socialist work of the Soviet Union.

To purchase the ticket to travel on the Trans-Siberian Railway to Vladivostok, the port of exit, one had to pay $200 to Intourist – and in dollars. (The price before this exodus began was only some $30.) While the money was "kosher" inside the office of Intourist, if

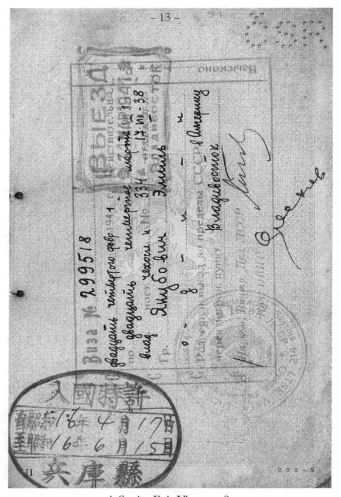

A Soviet Exit Visa, 1938.

caught with dollars on the street, Siberia would be the punishment.

Rav Avraham Kalmanowitch, the representative of the Mirrer Yeshiva and member of the *Vaad Hatzalah* (Rescue Committee) in New York, worked feverishly seven days a week, even on *Shabbos*, to collect money for the *yeshiva* boys before their permits expired. Some refugees sold clothes or valuables on the black market to raise the required money, even though doing so was very dangerous.

The Red Army sweeping back into Lithuania, June 14, 1940.

Moreover, it was forbidden to leave Russia with any valuables.[8]

Exit permits were eventually given to several thousand refugees, although the motivation for that remains a mystery to this day. Excluded, however, were Jews with Lithuanian citizenship – for they were now considered Russians – and others whom they chose to deport to Siberia for various reasons. By December they began to drag people out of bed in the middle of the night for deportation, among them religious and political leaders, and many so-called "undesirables." As for American visas, whoever was fortunate enough to obtain one did so with much difficulty and stress. Some refugees, therefore, chose to try the American Embassy in Moscow on their way to Japan, while others did so upon their arrival in Japan, but with little success. So for my father and me, Australia would become our alternative – a choice that in the end was well rewarded.

On October 6, 1940, Laurence Steinhardt, the American Jewish ambassador in Moscow, sent the following discouraging telegram to the State Department:

8. Kranzler, *The Japanese*, pp. 356–57.

I assume the (State) Department is aware of the fact that the Japanese visas were issued to these individuals (refugees) on the basis of assurances made to the Japanese legation in Kaunas by the Dutch Consul at the instance of the representative of the Joint Distribution Committee, that entrance visas to the Dutch possessions in the Americas were not required. . . . Each of the applicants thus far examined by the Embassy in Moscow regarded his Japanese transit visa . . . as merely a means of . . . entering the United States and remaining there for at least the duration of the war.[9]

Then came the final step that virtually terminated the issuing of American Visas. On June 5, 1941, the State Department sent a cable to its embassies instructing them to refuse visas to refugees with "children, parents, husband, wife, brothers, or sisters in controlled (German) territory." In the cable, the Department expressed their suspicion that this immigration might be the pretext for the infiltration of German and Russian spies. Since most Jewish refugees in Vilna by November 1940 still had no visas, they were resigned to remain in Vilna, in the hope that they would rejoin their loved ones left behind under German occupation.

By mid-August 1940, the *Rebbe*, the *Rebbetzin*, my aunt Sarah and my three younger uncles, Yisroel, Dovid and Hershel finally left Vilna. To set out to the States with his family, the *Zeide* needed large sums of money which he did not have. A letter from my uncle Moshe, my father's brother, who had already arrived in New York from Portugal, states that besides the two hundred dollars which the *Rebbe* received from his brother-in-law in Belgium, he borrowed at least a thousand more from several people in Vilna. Many *Chassidim* and others accompanied them to the station where they set out for Moscow and then for Vladivostok and Japan on the Trans-Siberian Railway. Finally on October 4, after a short stop in Japan, they sailed from Yokohama to the United States. The *Rebbe* was among the first in Vilna to get a U.S visa.[10]

---

9. Quoted in Phillips, *Flight and Rescue*, p. 87.

10. Phillips, *Flight and Rescue*, p. 135; Moshe sent numerous letters to my father when

```
- 3 - 1296, October 6, 2 p.m. from Moscow

cursory interrogation. However, as all of the members
of the groups that have thus far passed through Mos-
cow were in possession of Japanese transit visas,
presumably the situation created by the brevity of
their stay in Moscow can be dealt with in Tokyo.
        I assume the Department is aware of the fact that
Japanese transit visas were issued to these indivi-
duals on the basis of assurances made to the Japanese
Legation in Kaunas by the Dutch Consul at the instance
of the representative of the Joint Distribution
Committee in Kaunas that entrance visas to the Dutch
possessions in the Americas were not required and
that approximately 2,000 Japanese transit visas of
this type were recently issued in Kaunas, specifying
on the face of the visa that the applicants were en
route to the Dutch possessions in the Americas.
Each of the applicants thus far examined by the Embassy
in Moscow regarded his Japanese transit visa marked
as en route to the Dutch possessions in the Americas as
merely a means of obtaining a Soviet exit visa and
transit across Japan with the intention of entering
the United States and remaining there for at least the
duration of the war.
                                STEINHARDT
PEG
```

American Ambassador in Moscow, October 6, 1940.

Shortly before the *Rebbe's* departure, on August 9 1940, *Rav* Chaim Ozer Grodzenski, *zt"l*, the *Rav* Haroshi of Vilna and the *Gadol Hador*, passed away. Thousands of Jews, including many refugees, among them distinguished *Rebbes*, came to pay their last respects.[11]

My father and I had already been in possession of the visas to

---

we lived in Melbourne, Australia.

11. *Rabbi Nachman Zakon*, The Jewish Experience: 2000 Years *(Shaar Press, 2002), pp. 173–74.*

My mother and brother, *H"yd*, in the Warsaw Ghetto, 1940.

Curacao and Japan since July 31, 1940. However, we had not yet acquired the Russian exit permit. Miraculously, we obtained an exit permit at the last minute, in the first week of February 1941. At first, the expiration date was January 26, 1941, and whoever was fortunate and got a permit had only three weeks to leave Russia. Staying beyond the expiration date meant Siberia or worse, as those leaving "Holy Russia" were considered traitors. In the end the Soviet

Levaya of *Rav* Chaim Ozer Grodzenski. 1940.

authorities extended the validity of the permits until February 10. By mid-February, 1941, we, as well as my uncles, Chaskel, Yitzchok, and Aunt Tzipora, finally left Vilna for Kobe, Japan.

Postcards from my mother continued to arrive from the Warsaw Ghetto through the agency of the Red Cross until July 1941. Although we were all stricken with despair each time we read another and still another, postcard, my father and I did not yet give up hope for a miracle. Perhaps she and Yisroel, my brother, would show up. Secondly, my father was still in mourning for his father, and he therefore preferred to delay his departure. Moreover, we were also waiting for a possible American visa. Ultimately, my uncles and aunt, as children of the *Rebbe*, got their American visas while waiting in Japan, from the *Rebbe* after he was already in New York.

In mid-February 1941, we boarded the train to Moscow, where we would transfer after a short two-day stay in the city, to the Trans-Siberian Railway for a ten-day journey to the Russian-Asian port city of Vladivostok. While we were in Moscow waiting for the Trans-Siberian, we saw, probably, the result of NKVD intimidation, Lenin's glass tomb in Red Square and went to the local theater to see Sholem Aleichem's *Tuvia the Milkman*. Possibly, this play was performed because of government approval of its socialist ideas. Thus

Amakusa Maru, 1941.

The Trans-Siberian Railway, 1941.

we left Poland and Europe for good, with our most precious and dear ones behind us in Hitler's bloody hands. We left with anxiety wondering what their fate would be. Would I ever see my mother and brother again?

On the way, we stopped in Birobidzhan, the so-called Jewish autonomous state, which was created by Russian dictator Joseph Stalin on May 7, 1934. This was his idea of a model Jewish state, an alternative to Zion and the Zionist movement. Although the Soviets tried to encourage Jews to leave other parts of Russia, especially European Russia, and move to Birobidzhan where they would become farmers, few settled in that remote territory near Vladivostok and of those who did, fewer still remained Jews. For the Soviets, language determined identity, and Yiddish was therefore the Jewish identity.[12]

Tired and exhausted from the ten-day train ride, in Vladivostok we boarded the small and uncomfortable *Amakusa Maru*, a Japanese cargo ship built by Germany in 1902. Marvin Tokayer notes that the refugees who boarded the boat were still frightened, because Soviet officials were also boarding with them. But as soon as the Soviets got off, after guiding the ship out into international waters, the refugees began to dance with joy. The ship, which was to be torpedoed at

---

12. Ismar Elbogen, *A Century of Jewish Life*, pp. 551–55; On the Soviets extension of permits, see *Jewish Telegraph Agency*, February 6, 1941.

Tsuruga Harbor, 1941.

the end of World War II by the U.S. Navy, struggled for three days through very rough seas, with us, the passengers, stretched on the floor like sardines, until we landed in Tsuruga, Japan. The Jewish Committee from Kobe Japan, known by its cable address JEW-COM, made all the rail and passport arrangements. Hundreds of *yeshiva* boys, mainly from Mir, arrived alongside us in Tsuruga. One such group of about 80 students came on a Friday after sundown and they refused to sign the landing papers because it was already *Shabbos*. In the end after some anxious moments with the authorities, the Committee head, Mr. Gerechter, signed with the word *Shabbos* for all the boys and was dubbed the "*Shabbos Goy.*"

After a short rest, we headed by train for Kobe, our destination, which we finally reached on March 3, 1941.[13]

Upon our arrival, we were once again warmly greeted by the Jewish Committee. For the first time in a long time, we all felt a sense of relief, free of fear of either the Germans or the Soviets. At the same time, our thoughts painfully and constantly reminded us of the fate of my mother and brother Yisroel, especially after July 1941, by which time the last contact with them through both the mail and the Red Cross, had been cut off.

---

13. Kranzler, *The Japanese*, pp. 313–14.

Refugees arrive in
Kobe, 1941.

Japanese
Newspaper
reporting
arrival of Jewish
refugees 1941.

The Amshinover *Rebbe*, *Rav* Shimonle, who was with us in Kobe, sent a cable to Vilna from there, which was intercepted by the Japanese censor. *Rav* Shimonle was called in for an explanation. His cable read: "Shisho Miskadshim b'Talis Echod." The explanation given the censor was that there was a religious question with regard to marriage of six people with one *talis*. The explanation was accepted. But the real message was to alert Vilna that six people can travel on one Japanese family visa.

Leo Hanin, of the Kobe Jewish community and a member of JEWCOM, reported on an interesting encounter between the Amshinover *Rebbe*, *Rav* Shmuel Shatzkes, the Lomzjer *Rav*, and *Rav* Shlomo Shapiro, with several generals and admirals of the Japanese

Kobe, Japan, 1930s.

Defense Department. The meeting took place in Tokyo in February 1941 at the request of the Department:

"The interrogation took place in the naval officers' club. Besides our group, two generals, two admirals, one Japanese Shinto priest were present. The conversation continued for approximately three hours . . . . The main speaker was *Rav* Kalish, the Amshinover *Rebbe*, who, when asked by the generals why the Germans hated the Jews, answered quietly and with dignity that the Germans hate everyone who is not blond and blue eyed. And besides that, they hate us because we are Asians just like you, the Japanese. I cannot say at this time whether the military liked the rabbi's answer. But I distinctly remember that the top general, prior to leaving the meeting, said: GO HOME TO KOBE AND DON'T WORRY. I now interpret DON'T WORRY as follows: the general meant to say that we, the Japanese, although allies with the Germans, will not treat you people like they do . . . Leo Hanin was present as the translator.[14]

14. Tokayer, *The Fugu Plan*, pp.136–37; David A. Mandelbaum, *From Lublin to Shanghai* (New York Mesorah, 2012), p. 215.

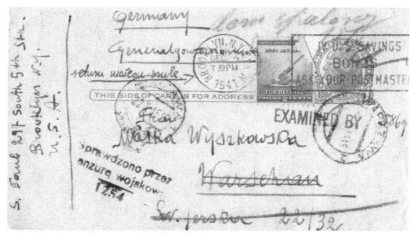

Undelivered postcard from the *Rebbe* to my mother

The Japanese attitude toward us, the refugees, was generally very favorable and sympathetic, on the part of both government officials and the public in Kobe. Although there was no lack of anti-Semitism in the Japanese government departments, on the whole, the ordinary citizen knew little about the Jew. Many senior government officials also remembered how a wealthy American Jew saved Japan from defeat during the Russo-Japanese war of 1904. The famous philanthropist Jacob Schiff was instrumental in organizing a total of five loans amounting to a sum of $196,250,000 – a huge sum in those days – that covered almost the entire Japanese war budget. Schiff's eagerness to help the Japanese, stemmed from his hatred of the fiercely anti-Semitic Czar Nicholas II and his cohorts in the Russian government. Nicholas II was the last of the Czars, and was responsible for the Kishinev pogroms of 1903–1905. Also, his support of the Black Hundreds, who barely let a month go by without an assault on some crowded Jewish community, was unreserved. These hoodlums galloped through towns and villages burning, pillaging, raping, and killing.[15]

---

15. Chaskel (Charles) Wyszkowski, *A Community in Conflict: American Jewry During the Great European Immigration* (New York: University Press of America, 1991), pp. 237–38; Tokayer, *The Fugu Plan*, p. 46.

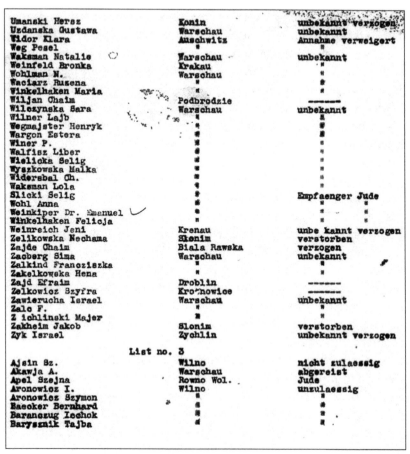

Umanski Hersz	Konin	unbekannt verzogen
Uzdanska Gustawa	Warschau	unbekannt
Vidor Klara	Auschwitz	Annahme verweigert
Weg Pesel	"	
Waksman Natalie	Warschau	unbekannt
Weinfeld Bronka	Krakau	"
Wohlman N.	Warschau	"
Waciarz Ruzena	"	"
Winkelhaken Maria	"	
Wiljan Chaim	Podbrodzie	-------
Wilczynska Sara	Warschau	unbekannt
Wilner Lajb	"	"
Wegmajster Henryk	"	"
Wargon Estera	"	"
Winer P.	"	"
Walfisz Liber	"	"
Wielicka Selig	"	"
Wyszkowska Malka	"	"
Widersbal Ch.	"	"
Waksman Lola	"	"
Slicki Selig	"	Empfaenger Jude
Wohl Anna	"	
Weinkiper Dr. Emanuel	"	" "
Winkelhaken Felicja	"	
Weinreich Jeni	Krenau	unbe kannt verzogen
Zelikowska Nechama	Slonim	verstorben
Zajde Chaim	Biala Rawska	verzogen
Zacberg Sima	Warschau	unbekannt
Zalkind Franciszka	"	"
Zakelkowska Hena	"	"
Zajd Efraim	Droblin	-------
Zelkowicz Szyfra	Krochowice	-------
Zawierucha Israel	Warschau	unbekannt
Zalo F.	"	"
Zichlinski Majer	"	"
Zakheim Jakob	Slonim	verstorben
Zyk Israel	Zychlin	unbekannt verzogen
	List no. 3	
Ajsin Sz.	Wilno	nicht zulaessig
Akawja A.	Warschau	abgereist
Apel Szejna	Rowno Wol.	Jude
Aronowicz I.	Wilno	unzulaessig
Aronowicz Szymon	"	"
Baecker Bernhard	"	"
Baranczug Icchok	"	"
Baryszmik Tajba	"	"

JDC List of Jews under German Occupation
Requesting Food Packages (my mother is listed as missing)

At the same time, the spread of anti-Semitism in Japan was partly generated by the Nazis, whose pact with Japan allowed them to exert increasing influence on government officials. They were particularly annoyed by the fact that Japan allowed and offered shelter to Jewish refugees in their country. In order not to jeopardize their relations with Germany, the Japanese tried to conduct all actions pertaining to the refugees on a low key. Moreover, the Japanese Foreign Ministry soon recognized that the outflow of refugees from Japan did not match the inflow which was steadily growing. In fact, at one point, the Japanese foreign minister Matsouka expressed his dismay. Speaking to Setsuzo Kotsuji, the only Hebrew-speaking Japanese, who was trying to help the refugees, he declared: "I had anticipated some trouble with the Germans by letting these people pass through Japan altogether. But now. . . . Do you know there are hundreds of Jews coming in every week, a torrent, a flood! And what is leaving? Virtually nothing. This was not my plan." Kotsuji, who later became a *ger*, borrowed a lot of money to bribe the Japanese officials to do his bidding.

In fact, as late as February–April, more and more refugees were still coming in, some even without a final destination altogether. But the "flood' finally came to a halt once the German invasion of Russia began on June 22, 1941. The Jews in Vilna were now trapped.

Earlier that month, the rabbis in Kobe, who were organized as a group, called on all refugees in the town to attend a mass prayer on June 12 at the *Beis Medrash*. In view of the growing threat by the Axis armies in North Africa to Eretz Israel, they felt prayer was very urgent. By mid-June, German and Italian divisions had reached El Alamein, Egypt, only 150 miles from Cairo.

Meanwhile, since Japanese transit visas were good for only three weeks and most of the refugees had as yet no place to go, the Japanese Foreign Office felt that a solution had to urgently be found. After a long and difficult discussion between Kotsuji and the Foreign Minister, Matsouka agreed to a proposal. It was decided that any question of visa extensions should be handled not by him and the Japanese government, but by the local officials in Kobe. This solution would be more discreet and less likely to come to the attention of the Germans.[16]

Kobe, the city where we stayed, was then the sixth largest in Japan, with a population of 1.5 million people including a tiny Jewish community of only 100 Jews. It also had a sizable western population made up mainly of businessmen. Even before our arrival, the local Jewish community sprang into action and paved the way with the help of the Joint Distribution Committee for all our immediate

---

16. Tokayer, *The Fugu Plan*, pp. 126–43; Abraham Kotsuji, *From Tokyo to Jerusalem* (New York: Geis Associates, 1964), pp. 163–64.

The Amshinover *Rebbe*, *Rav* Shatzkes, *Rav* Shapiro with Jewish and Japanese officials, 1941. *(Courtesy of YIVO Archives)*

needs, primarily accommodation. These Jews, who were very generous, had originally come in the 1930s from Russia. My father and I, as well as my uncles and aunt, moved into a house on Kumutchi Kochuma Street, which was situated on a mountainside.

We slept on a straw floor and were covered with a quilt. Our accommodations were not unusual for pre-war Japan. Japanese homes would often be bereft of furniture, as a precaution against frequent earth tremors. Rice bread rations were supplied in a truck each morning thus sparing us the need to stand in line with the Japanese inhabitants. One day, my father and uncle Chaskel came back from the market with a large five-foot fish that they prepared for supper in a sweet and sour sauce. It was a good treat. Often we had fish and vegetables for our meals. Matzos and wine from the States arrived just in time for Pesach.

Meanwhile, our transit visa was expiring, although it had been extended several times. Jewish organizations, both in New York and in Kobe were working desperately to get us out of Japan to some final destination. Few were able to get a visa to the U.S. As for Palestine,

Jewish Community headquarters ("Jewcom"), Kobe, 1941.

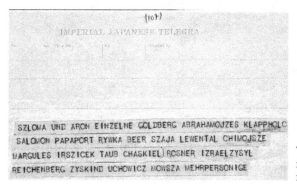

Telegram from Kobe requesting visas for my uncles, 1941.

since October 1940, the British no longer issued Certificates. Some individuals ended up travelling to Afghanistan or India.

By mid-August 1941, the Japanese authorities ordered all refugees who had no destination visa to leave Japan and transfer to Shanghai on the Chinese mainland. My uncles Chaskel and Yitzchok and Aunt Tzipora, under the name Taub, were eventually the last who were able to leave for the States and as children, to join the *Rebbe* in New York. My father and I, however, were not able to do so.

Fortunately, we received an affidavit from the Cohn family, cousins of my father, who had settled in Perth, Australia in 1936. Equipped with these papers, my father went ahead and obtained a visa from the Australian consul. Initially, my father, having sensed the looming Nazi threat way back in 1936 when still in Warsaw, was

AMERICAN CONSULATE
YOKOHAMA, JAPAN
JUNE 28, 1941.

NOTICE
FOR INFORMATION OF VISA APPLICANTS

ALL VISAS FOR ENTRY INTO THE UNITED STATES MUST
HEREAFTER RECEIVE THE APPROVAL OF THE UNITED STATES DEPARTMEI
OF STATE BEFORE THEY CAN BE ACTED UPON BY CONSULAT
OFFICERS.
CERTAIN FORMS HAVE BEEN PREPARED BY THE STATE
DEPARTMENT WHICH MUST BE EXECUTED BY THE VISA APPLICANT'S
SPONSORS IN THE UNITED STATES.
SUCH VISA APPLICANTS SHOULD THEREFORE REQUEST THEIR
SPONSORS IN THE UNITED STATES TO OBTAIN THESE FORMS FROM THE
STATE DEPARTMENT AND FILL THEM IN.
AFTER APPROVAL OF THE CASE BY THE AUTHORITIES IN
WASHINGTON THE STATE DEPATMENT WILL NOTIFY THE CONSUL WHO
WILL THEN ASK THE VISA APPLICANT TO COME TO HIS OFFICE.

U.S. Embassy "closing the gates" in Japan, 1941.

able to arrange all the papers for travel to Australia. But when the
Rebbe was confronted with the prospect of my mother, his daughter,
leaving for Australia before the War, he was in shock and regretfully
rejected the idea. So my father, went ahead that year, and offered the
papers to his cousins, the Cohns, who sailed for Australia. It was they
who now came to our rescue.

Chapter IV

Australia

O N JULY 6, 1941, shortly after Hitler invaded Russia (June 22), we, finally said goodbye to Japan and boarded the Japanese vessel, the *Kasima Maru*, for a month-long trip to Sydney, Australia.

The liner carried 60 passengers, including the new Japanese Consul-General to Australia and his family. Among the passengers there were 24 Jewish refugees, including my father and me. There was also a 23-year-old refugee stowaway, Hersch Rosenberg, originally from Warsaw, who was not discovered until the *Kasima Maru* had docked in Sydney. He had hidden in a lifeboat when we left Kobe and stayed there for two or three days. Later he slept under a bunk in one of the cabins and then occupied a spare bunk in still another cabin. He was thus able to escape detection throughout the trip. All the refugees were given permits to leave Japan by the Japanese authorities and entry visas by the Australian ambassador to Tokyo. We took along rice bread from Kobe but after only two days, perhaps because of the sea air, it had spoiled and we threw it overboard. At first, the ship sailed directly south without incident and after some two weeks docked in Manila, the capital of the Philippines. While in Manila, we disembarked and my father purchased a bagful of pineapples, a very popular fruit on the island. After a short stay, the ship resumed her course heading south to Australia.

However, as soon as the ship passed the southern tip of the Philip-

Kasima Maru, 1941.

Manilla 1940.

pines, she suddenly began to swing around in an easterly direction. She was originally scheduled to sail through the Dutch islands of Borneo, Java, and Sumatra, now Indonesia. Word that the ship was heading in the wrong direction and away from Australia quickly spread among the passengers. Our anxiety grew after the captain refused to meet a delegation of the passengers. We had suspected that

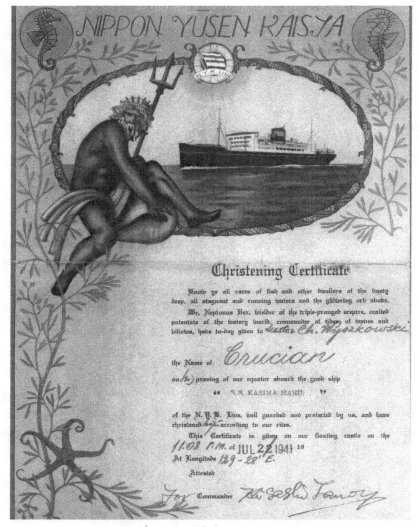

My certificate, awarded to passengers, 1941.

they were possibly planning to dump us on some deserted island. The night passed, shrouded in mystery and suspense, while the ship continued on her easterly course and in total blackout.

In the meantime, we later found out, that newspapers in Australia had reported the delay and possible disappearance of the *Kasima Maru*. They began to speculate on her whereabouts. Several papers

NO NEWS OF LINER

Kasima Maru Overdue

The Japanese liner Kasima Maru has not been reported since her licence to load cargo at Townsville was withdrawn, while she was off the Australian coast.

News of the Kasima Maru is awaited with great interest since the new Consul-General for Japan, Mr. Itsoo Goto, his staff, and the second secretary at the Legation in Canberra, Mr. Sakashima, are passengers. There are many European passengers on the vessel.

Nothing has been heard of the liner during the week, and it is thought that she may be steaming to a Japanese port.

The agents for the Kasima Maru said yesterday that they had received no message. They would have expected one if she had intended to berth to-day.

It is still possible that she may arrive in port without warning, and arrangements have been made for her to berth to-day.

Originally it was understood that the liner would call both at Townsville and Brisbane.

FREIGHTER OVERDUE

The Japanese freighter China Maru did not arrive in Sydney yesterday, although she was overdue from South Australia.

Her agents expected that she would arrive after the freighter Canberra Maru had loaded 700 bales of wool and left port.

A large cargo of wool was waiting on the wharf for the China Maru, but it is now thought likely that she is making direct for Japan.

CANBERRA MARU SAILS

The freighter Canberra Maru sailed from Sydney yesterday after adding 700 bales of wool to her cargo of wheat and flour.

Export of this cargo was authorised because it had been paid for before Japanese credits were frozen.

The Canberra Maru berthed on Wednesday, after standing off the coast for nearly 24 hours.

She was to have loaded 1,200 sheep, but they were not shipped. The wheat on board was from South Australia, and the flour from Victoria.

The vessel also carried a number of passengers, chiefly Japanese business men. Others on board included Japanese women and children.

Miss B. D. Campbell, of Melbourne, who has been appointed confidential secretary to the Australian Minister to Japan, Sir John Latham, was also a passenger.

Miss Campbell said that she hoped to remain in Japan long enough to see a great deal of it and of its people. She expects to be away at least 12 months.

She added that she had been given much helpful advice about Japan by members of the Japanese Legation in Australia.

KASIMA MARU STILL SILENT

No news of the Japanese liner Kasima Maru (10,000 tons) was received yesterday in Sydney.

The Kasima Maru was due in Sydney last Friday, but did not arrive. She also missed calls at Thursday Island and Townsville without sending radio advice.

Passengers in the Kasima Maru include the newly-appointed Japanese Consul-General to Australia (Mr. Itsoo Goto) and his family.

A Sydney representative of the agents for the Nippon Yusen Kaisha line, owners of the Kasima Maru, said yesterday: "We have had no word. She was due on Friday. I can't say more."

When it was suggested that the liner was on her way back to Japan, the official repeated his previous answer.

The Minister for External Affairs (Sir Frederick Stewart) said last night that he had not heard from Mr. Goto, and knew nothing of the whereabouts of the Kasima Maru.

Report on missing liner, August 1, 1941. (*The Sydney Morning Herald*)

suggested that she might have received a directive from the home office, in view of the war preparations, and headed back to a Japanese port. Others expected the ship's ultimate arrival in Australia, especially since she carried the new Japanese ambassador and his family. All this was happening without anyone suspecting an imminent Japanese attack. Four months later, on December 7, the American fleet at Pearl Harbor was struck with a massive onslaught from the Japanese Imperial Airforce, which came as a complete surprise to America. Within hours, the entire fleet lay in ruins and the war against Japan began.

One early morning, we heard the sound of an approaching plane. Breathlessly, we all rushed up to the deck, and to our relief it turned out to be a Dutch reconnaissance aircraft. After spotting the *Kasima Maru*, which it apparently was sent out to find, the plane began to fly very low over and around the ship. Instinctively, we waved to the pilot, an action that drew hostile looks from the crew on deck, who appeared ready to throw us all overboard. But no sooner was the plane gone, than a Dutch destroyer appeared on the horizon

Destroyer Stops Japanese Ship

Blacked Out, Names Removed: Reaches Sydney 8 Days Late

SYDNEY.—During the voyage to Australia of the Japanese liner Kasima Maru, it was stopped and examined by a Dutch destroyer. This was revealed today when the vessel reached Sydney, eight days behind schedule.

Passengers told how the Kasima Maru was blacked out at night and had all Japanese signs painted out. It drifted aimlessly to the north of Australia before it turned as if heading back to Japan.

THE Kasima Maru carried the new Consul-General for Japan (Mr. Goto).

Once the liner moved to the north, as though heading for Japan, then towards the east as though the Carolines were the objective. In the meantime the passengers were warned against making light signals on deck at night.

Mr. Goto asked for "news of the outside world" from his first interviewer, and then he said, "My Government would not have sent me to Sydney if there were going to be war."

Polish Escapees

Carrying 52 Poles, who escaped across Russia to Japan following the Nazi invasion; three Britons, who have been living in Japan; and four Japanese, the Kasima Maru left Kobe on July 6, called at Manila on July 14, was at Davao on July 17, and then went into the blue. She was due at Thursday Island on July 24, but on that date was somewhere near the Equator.

There were no charts displayed and the Japanese officers were uncommunicative. The Poles believed they were somewhere round Dutch territorial waters, at one stage about 100 miles west of New Guinea.

The Kasima Maru, according to Mr. F. W. Mackie, chartered accountant, of Kobe, started to go north the day before she was due at Thursday Island. "I got up in the morning, and found the sun pouring into my window," he said. "This was unusual, for I was not on the sunny side.

"A Little Anxious"

"We were cruising about for five days, and then we turned south again, and we thought that we were going to move in a general easterly direction towards the Carolines. We certainly headed in that direction for a while.

"Some of the Poles were panicky; but the other Britons and I were quite calm but a little anxious. We knew we were safe, but did not like the prospect of going back to Japan.

"Then one morning at 7.30 three planes roared out towards us, and at 10 a.m. the grey shape of a warship was seen low down on the horizon.

"It was a Dutch destroyer. It came close and lowered a boat. Between 20 and 30 sailors and officers came alongside the Kasima Maru and boarded her for examination.

"The Poles crowded the rails anxiously. They had hopes of the Dutch destroyer taking them off. For about half an hour the Dutch officers were with the captain, and soon afterwards the Kasima Maru turned at full speed for the south and did not sight land until she arrived off Sydney.

Japanese Packing

MELBOURNE—All Japanese members of the staff of commercial firms in Melbourne, except possibly for one or two, will leave next week for Japan.

There were about 30 Japanese in business in Melbourne. Wives and families of Japanese living here have already left. Some returned months ago.

In one large Japanese firm today, not one Japanese member of the staff was at work. They were all busy arranging passages and packing.

Since the "freezing" order last Satur-

Kasima Maru ship
intercepted,
August 1941, Australia.
(*The Sydney Morning Herald*)

and began to close in on the *Kasima Maru* with her guns pointed at the ship. We held our breath for some anxious moments as signals were exchanged between the two vessels. Within minutes a Dutch armed military detachment boarded our ship, wrested control from the Japanese, swung it round to a southern direction, and sailed her all the way to Sydney, Australia.[1]

Based on the available sources, the entire episode seems to have been the result of ongoing tension between Japan and Australia. Australian dockworkers had refused to unload Japanese vessels, and money for cargo consisting of Japanese machinery and other merchandise was held frozen in escrow accounts. It is also possible that the ship received signals from its home base to dump us on some island in the Pacific and return quickly to their home base as a precaution on the eve of war. It now also seems pretty clear that

---

1. *Sydney Morning Herald*, August 1, 1941, p. 7.

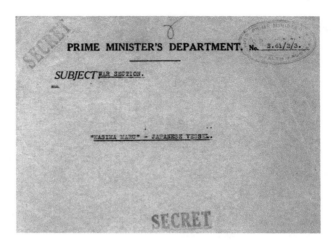

the Japanese were already preparing for the war against the United States and their surprise attack on Pearl Harbor.

We arrived in Sydney on Saturday night, August 9, 1941, thus ending a thirty-four-day drama full of suspense. As for the Jewish stowaway, he was allowed to disembark with the rest of us, after the intervention of the Polish consul. We finally all heaved a sigh of relief.[2]

Sydney, where we disembarked on Saturday night, August 9, 1941, is a beautiful city of almost 4.4 million people, best known for its harbor-front Opera House and the towering arched Harbour Bridge. Upon our arrival, we were invited to the home of Rabbi Harry Mordechai Freedman, who translated into English many volumes of the Soncino edition of the Talmud, and we stayed there for the night. The next morning we took the train for a 500-mile trip to Melbourne, Victoria, which we expected to become our permanent home. Rated as the most livable city in the world for the fifth year in a row, also with a population of 4.4 million like Sydney, Melbourne is a leading financial center and was for many years, the capital of Australia.

Upon our arrival in the city of Melbourne, we were given a very warm reception in the Kadima Hall by a special committee. Among

---

2. *Advocate*, August 11, 1941; *Argus*, August 11, 1941.

LEGATION OF JAPAN

BRANCH CHANCELLERY
MELBOURNE, C.1.

6th August, 1941.

My dear Prime Minister,

      I desire to inform you that the
S.S. "Kasima Maru" is expected to arrive in Sydney
from Japan on or about the 7th August, with about
837 tons of cargo on board, consisting mainly of
machine tools, silk yarn, silk and artificial silk
piece goods, and tinned salmon and crab. The
value of the cargo is approximately ¥3,000,000.

      As you are well aware, the above-
mentioned cargo was shipped from Japan, in fulfil-
ment of orders of customers in Australia, before
the present situation arose. If the money in
payment for the above-mentioned goods is to be
frozen in Australia, the shippers in Japan will
suffer the whole of the loss, and they are inclined
to contend that the goods should be brought back
to Japan without being landed at Australian ports.

      You are no doubt also aware that
there are some outstanding Japanese orders for
Australian primary products, payment for which is
rendered unpracticable owing to the recent freezing
of Japanese balances in the British Empire.

      I venture to enquire, under instructions
from my Government, whether your Government will grant
special consideration to the case of the above-
mentioned cargo, and permit the shipment to Japan
of such primary products as wool or wheat under
contract up to the value of the cargo in question,
in order that the matter of payment in Japan may be
settled.

      I shall be very much obliged if you
will inform me of your Government's decision on this
matter at the earliest possible moment, since the
necessary instructions must be given to the vessel
in order that unnecessary complications may be
avoided.

                      Yours faithfully,

                          Satume Kawai

                      Japanese Minister.

The Rt. Hon. R. G. Menzies, K.C.,
    Prime Minister,
        Commonwealth of Australia,
            Commonwealth Offices,
                Treasury Gardens, MELBOURNE.

COPY SENT TO MINR & DEPT. CUSTOMS
          "   "   COMMERCE.
             7/8/41.

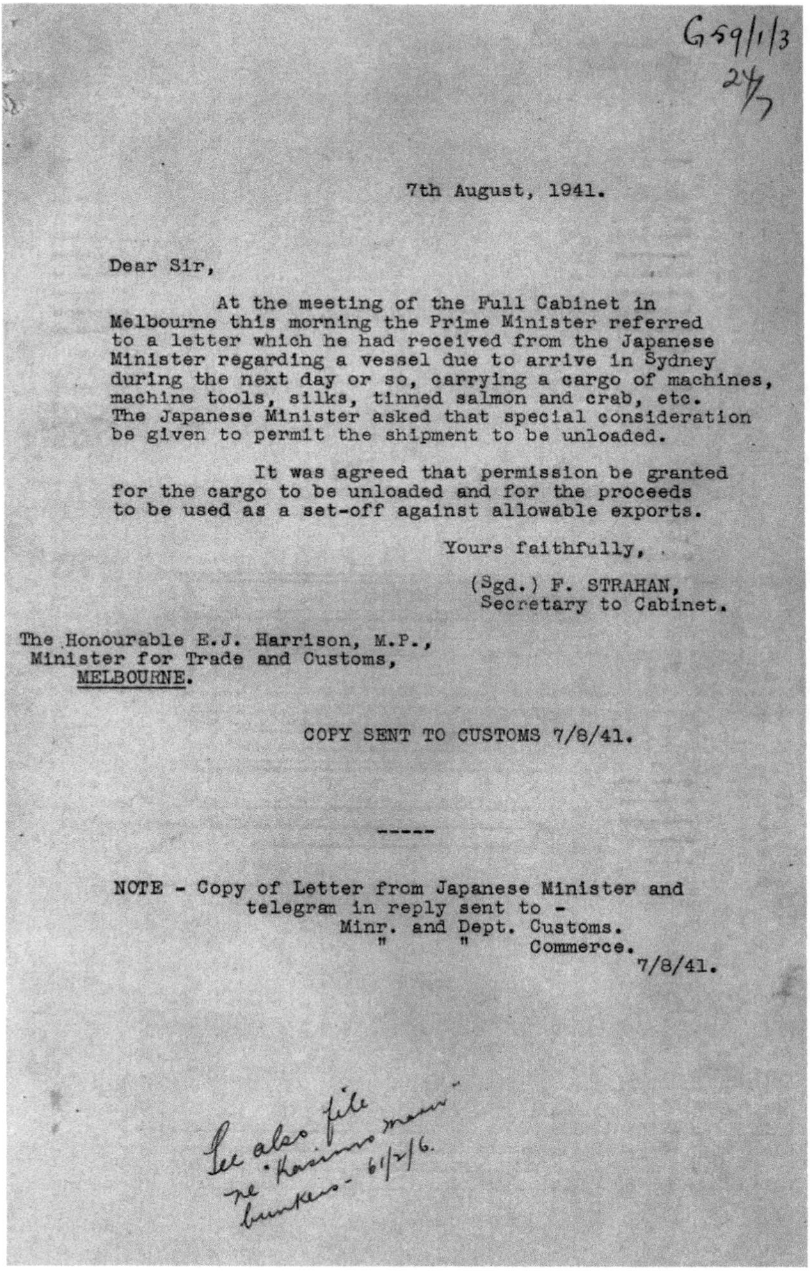

G 59/1/3
24/7

7th August, 1941.

Dear Sir,

At the meeting of the Full Cabinet in
Melbourne this morning the Prime Minister referred
to a letter which he had received from the Japanese
Minister regarding a vessel due to arrive in Sydney
during the next day or so, carrying a cargo of machines,
machine tools, silks, tinned salmon and crab, etc.
The Japanese Minister asked that special consideration
be given to permit the shipment to be unloaded.

It was agreed that permission be granted
for the cargo to be unloaded and for the proceeds
to be used as a set-off against allowable exports.

Yours faithfully,

(Sgd.) F. STRAHAN,
Secretary to Cabinet.

The Honourable E.J. Harrison, M.P.,
Minister for Trade and Customs,
  MELBOURNE.

COPY SENT TO CUSTOMS 7/8/41.

NOTE - Copy of Letter from Japanese Minister and
          telegram in reply sent to -
              Minr. and Dept. Customs.
                "   "   Commerce.
                              7/8/41.

*See also file
"Kasima maru"
bunkers - 61/2/6.*

Declassified documents on *Kasima Maru*, August 1941.

Sydney Harbour, prewar, circa 1930s.

Collins Street, Melbourne 1940s.

the guests who addressed the arriving refugees was the Polish consul who came especially from Sydney to greet us.

According to the 2016 census, the Jewish population of Australia, is about 91,000, although the Israeli newspaper *Haaretz* estimates it to be closer to 150,000, of whom about 45,000 live in Melbourne.

Australian Jews are, by and large, *Ashkenazim*, and are divided into Orthodox, Conservative, and Reform. However, according to Dr. Suzanne Rutland, most Australian Jews can best be described as non-practicing orthodox. The 1940s also saw a rise, for the first time, of ultra-Orthodox Judaism including a very active number of Chabad in Melbourne and Sydney. There are nineteen Jewish day schools, the two largest of which are Moriah College in Sydney, with 1800 students, and Mount Scopus in Melbourne, with 1500 students. The ultra-Orthodox community established its own schools.

In 1941, when we came to Melbourne, few schools could be found suitable for me. Although I went every day to the Hascola Talmud Torah, much of my Torah learning, especially *Gemara*, I did with my father, almost as a daily routine. Learning in the Talmud Torah was clearly not the same as in Warsaw. Nevertheless, as soon as my father and I settled down, I was able to make friends, and pretty soon we found ourselves busy studying together. For secular studies, I attended, a regular government school, as did other students. In a relatively short time, both my father and I were able to acquire a fairly good knowledge of English, a language that was a key to normal life in this new environment. My childhood was rapidly disappearing and I was developing a more mature outlook on the world around me. Thoughts of my mother and brother Yisroel and their struggle for survival often kept me awake at night.

Late at night, when shortwave radio reception had improved, I

Reception of Jewish Refugees at Kadima Hall, Melbourne, August 1941. (*Jewish Archives, Kadimah, Carlton*)

Former home of Hascola Talmud Torah, Carlton, 1941.

would spend many hours during the four war years trying to catch the BBC World Service, in the hope of getting news from distant Europe. Little did we know that even this, like most other radio stations, would have nothing to offer us about what was really happening with our brothers and sisters under the Nazi heel.

During those early years in Melbourne, my father was depressed and despondent. Moreover, letters from the *Rebbe*, my *Zeide*, and my uncle Moshe, who by the end of January 1941, were already in New York, kept arriving almost every week, but there was little, if anything, from the Warsaw Ghetto that would offer some comfort. Virtually all communication with our brothers and sisters was cut off for good. Occasionally, these letters from New York would offer us, in bits and pieces, indirect flashes on some of the ghastly reports about the mass executions and gassings in the death camps.[3]

To the best of my knowledge, my uncle Moshe had been in Paris on business when the war broke out. Information provided by his

3. Letters in my possession from my *Zeide*, the *Rebbe*.

grandson David Wyszkowski, however, differs somewhat. He insists that Nathan (David's father), was already there as a university student. It was he, my cousin explained, who finally convinced my uncle to come to France early in August before the German invasion of Poland, by suggesting that the waters in Vichy would bring relief to his wife who was suffering from arthritis in her legs. Instead of returning later to Warsaw, they took flight, as soon as the Germans began their invasion of France, with my aunt Dora and their two sons, Nathan and Freddie, and reached Portugal through Spain. In order to get a transit visa from the Spanish Consul, they first had to travel to Bordeaux, where they also obtained a visa for Portugal from the Portuguese Consul. He was very sympathetic to Jews (the rumor was that he was a descendant of a Marrano family) and granted them hundreds of visas. Since the State Department, by then, had made it impossible to get a visa to the United States, they saved their lives by the age-old method of bribery. Unfortunately, being Polish Jews, they could not possibly match the hefty bribes offered by the many wealthy German Jews who had reached the American consul in Lisbon ahead of them. So they went to a smaller consulate in Aporto, northern Portugal, where they bribed the American Consul. Finally, they all boarded the SS *Nyassa* in Lisbon in April, 1941, for New York.

As soon as Uncle Moshe arrived in New York, he began sending food packages to Warsaw. According to a letter of July 27, 1941, he sent as many as thirty packages of food. Moreover, in a still later letter dated May 25, 1942, Uncle Moshe writes: "Next week I shall have another opportunity to help Malka [my mother]!"[4] Letters from my mother dated April 19 and July 6, 1941 confirmed receipt of these packages. However, his plan of May 25, 1942 probably never came to fruition, as all communication with Nazi Poland had been severed before the end of 1941.

To add to our misfortune, by the end of that year, another troubling thought raised deep concern. The Japanese attack on Pearl Harbor, brought fears of war to the Australian shores as well, and the possibility of a Japanese landing somewhere on the long north

---

4. Letters from Moshe Wyszkowski, New York, 1941–42.

Former home of Beth David Hebrew Congregation
(also known as the Stone Shul), where I celebrated my Bar Mitzvah, 1943.

Australian coast. Now that we were in Australia, we began to share the worries of all Australians.

Meanwhile, my father who was a great *talmid chochom*, began looking for a job. But here too, in this new world, he once again declined a rabbinical post which he was offered.

We had arrived in Australia shortly before Pearl Harbor and the outbreak of hostilities in the Pacific. This soon drew Australia into the war, which immediately affected everybody. Jobs became scarce. Consequently, my father, especially as a newcomer with little knowledge of English, had very little choice. He therefore accepted an offer from a wealthy industrialist manufacturing woolen blankets, to be a night watchman in one of his plants. During the day, when he was not engaged in learning with me or on his own, he prepared kits which contained sheets of metal for potmenders, popularly used during the war to repair pots. These jobs must have been very boring and perhaps even humiliating for him. But during the war years, any job was acceptable and he was happy to earn some money, the first since September 1939.

Meanwhile, on November 25, 1943, we celebrated my Bar Mitzvah at the Beth David Hebrew Congregation, 12 Pitt Street, Carlton, Melbourne. I read *Parshas Vayishlach*, the portion of the week,
and delivered a short *droshe* (speech or sermon).

Although my *Zeide*, the *Rebbe*, was in debt to several people from
Vilna, for the money without which he could have never made it
to America with his family, he took the trouble to send us *matzohs*
for Pesach and *tefillin* for my Bar Mitzvah. As is the custom, I also
received many gifts, including a gold watch on a chain, which I received from our very good and wealthy friend Mr. Liebler, and fit
into my vest pocket. But I guess that watch was not meant to be. I
returned it promptly upon my father quoting the famous life lesson
from Proverbs, "He Who Hates Gifts will Live."[5] Although my Bar
Mitzvah was celebrated as required, this event, in the absence of my
dear mother and brother, was quite subdued.

As time went by, my father, who had been averse to a rabbinical
post, slowly became involved in Jewish community affairs. First he
began to deliver a *droshe* on the *parsha* of the week almost every *Shabbos*, in the Stone Talmud Torah. I recently published a collection of
his *droshes* under the title משכן אברהם.[6] Moreover, as the reports of the
Nazi atrocities escalated, my father broke his silence. He decided to
take the initiative and organize a rescue fund similar to the Joint in
the States. Consequently, he went public and made several speeches
on the bloodbaths in Hitler's torture chambers. His speeches drew
large crowds, and in 1943, the United Jewish Relief Fund was inaugurated.

The Fund was a success from the start and drew much support
from the Jewish community and to some extent from the general
public as well. People gave generously and the money was forwarded
to the American Joint Distribution and Vaad Hatzalah organizations
in support of their rescue operations. At the same time, my father
also began for the first time a weekly column that appeared in the
local Jewish paper, די יידישע נייעס.

During these war years, we resided in Carlton, which became

---

5. Proverbs 15:27.

6. אברהם וויישקובסקי, משכן אברהם, ירושלים: אות הזהב, 2006.

the center of activity for most of the Orthodox community. *Shuls*, *Shtiblech*, Talmud Torahs, and other Jewish institutions all found their place in that district of Melbourne. Among the people I remember who stood shoulder high, was the great educator and *talmid chochom*, *Rav* Chaim Dov-Ber Silver, whom I met again several years later in Jerusalem, where he made his final and permanent home. I also remember *Rav* Mordechai Eizen, who spent many years at the Carlton Talmud Torah, tirelessly educating Jewish children. While growing up in Australia, thanks to their talent, vision, and effort, many young men, friends of mine, like Shlomo Slonim and Yehuda Gor, were among the first to find the right path in Judaism. They moved on to advanced learning in Telshe Yeshiva, Cleveland and other places, among the best *yeshivas* in America. Since the early war years, and with the influx of several distinguished rabbis from the famous *yeshivas* in Poland as well as some from German Jewry, the Jewish community, especially Orthodoxy, gained momentum and began to thrive.[7]

By 1945, with the war finally coming to an end, it gradually became crystal clear what to expect. We were confronted with the bitter truth in all its monstrosity. Except for some walking skeletons and survivors half alive/half dead who emerged from the death camps, European Jewry went up in smoke and vanished. My mother, brother, and many relatives and friends, were never to be seen again. We, on the other hand, with HASHEM's help, miraculously survived.

Both my *Zeide*, the *Rebbe*, and my Uncle Moshe, began to urge my father to join them in the United States. Uncle Moshe also suggested that, perhaps, he should consider marriage. Moreover, he did his best, through the mail, to lift my father's spirit. After December 1941, when mail and food packages could no longer be sent from the States to Warsaw, he tried to make some arrangement by contacting a friend in neutral Switzerland and also in Lisbon, Portugal.

At the end of November, 1947, we received very sad news. My *Zeide*, the Modzitzer *Rebbe*, *z"tl*, Harav Shaul Yedidya Elozor, passed

---

7. Shmuel Gorr, "From Kelme to Melbourne," *Yiddishkeit* 1986; David J. Havin, *Jewish Carlton Comes to Life*, Oz Torah, 2007.

Telegram reporting the passing of the Rebbe, December 1947.

away. His departure came on a historic day. That day, November 29, the United Nations General Assembly in Lake Success, New York, adopted a majority resolution on the partition of Palestine in favor of the establishment of a Jewish state. At the last minute the *Rebbe* was able to hear the good news for which he had prayed all his life. The last time I had seen him was in Vilna in 1940.

He will be remembered among the *Gedolei Hador* by us all, for his Torah and world renowned *neginah* compositions and for his brave endorsement, with few reservations, through his Torah, of all major efforts by religious and non-religious factions in rebuilding the *Yishuv*. He was one of the few famous *Rebbes* to have been completely convinced of the urgency of a political solution that would ultimately lead to the establishment of a Jewish state in *Eretz Yisrael*. He will also be remembered as a loving and devoted father and *zeide*. My uncle in Tel Aviv, *Rav* Shmuel-Eliyahu Taub, his firstborn, succeeded him as *Rebbe*.

The funeral procession brought the *Rebbe* to his final resting place on *Har Hazesim*. He was the last to have been buried there for many years. Despite the real risk of Arab assaults on the highway, the funeral took place and thousands went up from Tel Aviv to Jerusalem. The procession was headed by the Chief Rabbis, Herzog and

The *Rebbe's matzeivah* on Har Hazesim, 1947.

Uziel, the Rabbis of Tel Aviv, Unterman and Toledano, as well as the Chazon Ish, who credited the *Rebbe* with saving the Mir and other *yeshivas* in Vilna, amongst many other rabbis.

By the end of 1946, I completed high school and began a program in communication engineering. Although I completed two years of this program, the rapid developments in the Middle East during 1948, with the birth of the State of Israel, changed my plans.

Chapter V

Israel

CTION AND THE MIND don't always work in harmony. And
so it was with me. Shortly after November 10, 1948, when
my father and I were at last granted British Nationality and
Australian Citizenship, I began to entertain thoughts of a change of
plans. I felt a strong urge and eagerness, now that I had also turned
19, to go to the newly born State of Israel and share in this great
moment of our people's glory.[1]

This great moment of birth, was preceded by a difficult "preg-
nancy," which began after World War I in 1918 and culminated with
great human sacrifice 30 years later in the War of Independence.
During the three years prior to that war, boatloads of Holocaust
survivors were struggling to leave the European continent, soaked
with oceans of Jewish blood. These vessels, mostly unsuitable for
human travel, were headed for Palestine, despite the embargo that
had then been imposed on reaching its shores by the British foreign
minister, Ernest Bevin.[2] Many of these desperate souls, who had just
been liberated from Hitler's concentration and death camps by the
Allied armies, were now turned back by the British forces, often even
before they could reach their destination, and put, once again, into

---

1. *Mendes-Flohr and Reinharz,* The Jew in the Modern World, *pp. 629–30.*

2. Walter Laqueur, *A History of Zionism* (Holt, Rinehart and Winston, New York, 1972),
pp. 565–67, 577.

MV *Georgic*, the ship I took to Liverpool, 1949.

internment camps on the neighboring island of Cyprus.[3]

Meanwhile, although my father was initially surprised by my plans to go it alone to Israel and was reluctant to support them, he came around in the end. Getting there, however, because of the embargo was, indeed, a problem. Finally, it was decided that the best way to circumvent the embargo was for me to first go to England as a student.

Finally, in February 1949, I left Australia for good, a country which I will never forget for having offered us such a warm welcome in a time of desperate need, and set out on my trip. After an enthusiastic send-off sponsored by the local Mizrachi organization, who viewed me as their first representative to go to Israel, and then kissing my father goodbye, I boarded the MV *Georgic* in Sydney (the city where I had arrived in Australia), for a month-long journey to Liverpool, England. The *Georgic*, which had a tonnage of some 40,000, had been converted from a naval vessel to a passenger ship. This was only the first leg of my trip. We stopped at Suez, Egypt, only a short distance from Israel, but I had to pretend along with some ten others from Australia, because of both the British and the Egyptian authorities, that I was headed for England to advance my education. The ship then set sail for Liverpool, England, where it docked a week later. I checked into a hotel for the night, and by the next morning I was already on a train to Southampton, where I boarded a ferry to Le Havre, France.

So here I was in the year 1949, back to post-war Europe, from where I had fled in 1941. The landscape has changed and signs of destruction were still visible. With few exceptions, European soil and rivers like the Danube, were soaked with innocent Jewish blood. By this time, however, six million *k'doshim*, including my mother,

---

3. Laqueur, *A History of Zionism*, p. 568.

SS *Kedmah*, the
ship I took to
Haifa, 1949.

brother uncles and aunts were dead. But so was also the great monster – Hitler – and his future plans. I was now on my way to the land of our dreams: Israel.

I took a train that brought me, after a long ride, to the southern French port city of Marseille, where I boarded the first 2,500-ton Israeli ship, the *Kedmah*, to Haifa, Israel.

On the first day, we organized a *minyan* for *Mincha*, but only nine men were available. So I asked one of the sailors on deck wearing a cap with a Magen David on it if he would join us to be the tenth, to which he readily agreed. Although he did not pray, he stood at the door where the *minyan* assembled. After concluding our prayers, I engaged him in a Hebrew conversation. To my surprise, he revealed that he was not Jewish, but a Catholic from Ireland who had joined Zim Lines many years ago.

The trip on the *Kedmah* was a pleasant one, and after a few days we arrived in Haifa. After a brief stay there, I boarded a bus directly to Tel Aviv where I soon found the residence of my uncle, *Rav* Shmuel-Eliyahu Taub, *zt"l*, who had succeeded my *Zeide* as the third Modzitzer *Rebbe*. His home at 31 Kfar Giladi Street, which was the *Rebbe's* first since settling in Israel, consisted of very modest living quarters and a *Shul*.

Since 1949, however, Modzitz has come a long way. Under the new *Rebbe*, *Rav* Chaim-Shaul Taub, the grandson of *Rav* Shmuel-Eliyahu, the House of Modzitz now has a larger following, and is much expanded and more spacious, consisting of two large buildings; one, the residence of the *Rebbe* and the other, the *Beis Medrash*.

Upon my arrival in 1949, both the *Rebbe*, *Rav* Shmuel-Eliyahu, and *Rebbetzin*, Rivka, greeted me with a hearty welcome, and despite the limited space, they did everything to accommodate me and make me feel at home. I stayed with them for about a week, and soon came to respect the *Rebbe* and how highly he valued hospitality. The door was always open and the *Rebbe* would welcome everyone with a smile no matter who it was. During my years in Israel, as a bachelor and later when I got married, I was a frequent visitor of the *Rebbe* and the *Rebbetzin* in Beit Modzitz, Tel Aviv.

Rav Shmuel-Eliyahu Taub, the new Modzitzer *Rebbe* at his desk, 1950.

My uncle, the new Modzitzer Rebbe, Rav Shmuel-Eliyahu Taub, 1949.

After the week had passed, I got in touch with Kibbutz Yavneh, and they agreed to admit me on a six month trial-basis as a temporary member. The founders of the kibbutz had come together in Germany as part of an alliance of religious pioneers who made *aliyah* in 1929. Two years later, they founded the Rodges Group in the village of Abraham, near Petach Tikva. The kibbutz finally moved in 1940–41 to its present location at Yavneh, on the coastal plain, some five miles to the west of the city of Rehovot. Yavneh is accepted today as the flagship of religious Zionist cooperatives in Israel, economically successful, and the bedrock for the *Yeshivot Hesder* (a combined program of learning and army service). Although agriculture is its cornerstone and much of its export, Yavneh is also proud of its canned meat production.

During my six month stay in the kibbutz, I was given a variety of jobs, some of which were physically easy, while others more difficult. On some days I was out in the field early in the morning picking tomatoes, grapes, and other fruits and vegetables. The work was pleasant, but the struggle with the particularly aggressive mosquitos, known locally as *barhash*, was quite uncomfortable. On other days I would help unload heavy sacks of either salt or flour from a platform, perhaps an excellent exercise for the muscles, but not great for the back. During those months, I was also involved in other work programs, including waiting at tables, as was expected in a kibbutz. I spent part of the time learning with and without a *chavrusa* (learning partner), as well as writing for the local newsletter. By and large, I must say that my experience in the kibbutz was a challenge physically and spiritually and I am not certain whether I would ever have been able to fully fit in.

Although a newcomer to this environment, I was well treated. Were it not for the fact that my entire family was elsewhere, including my father, the experiment would certainly have been more tempting. I very much enjoyed my six month stay in Yavneh, but the socialist idea of collectivism did not quite seem to fit into my weltanschauung.[4]

Meanwhile, in view of my departure for Israel as well as the earlier encouragement of the *Zeide*, before he died, and Uncle Moshe urging my father to join them in New York, the issue of my father's departure to America became more relevant. So my father began preparations for travel from Australia to New York. Initially, he had planned to leave for the States shortly after the war in June 30, 1946, even before we became Australian citizens, but he had postponed the idea. Finally, almost a year after my departure, he boarded the RMS *Orcades* in November 1949 and after transferring in Southampton, England, to the *Queen Elizabeth*, he sailed for New York, where he arrived on December 7.

---

4. מ. אורליאן, הקיבוץ הדתי והתפתחותו, תל-אביב: הוצאת הקיבוץ הדתי, תש"ו אהובה לבל, הציונות הדתית (ירושלים: הוצאת אמי"ת, תש"נ), דפים 96–194.
Yonina Talmon, Family and Community in the Kibbutz (Cambridge, MA: Harvard University Press).

Kibbutz Yavneh, 1949.

Kibbutz Yavneh, 1949.

As my six month period in the kibbutz was approaching its end, my thoughts shifted to returning to school, for which I was becoming very eager. During my stay on the kibbutz, I had been able to advance my knowledge of Hebrew, and thus better prepared to continue my education in Israel.

As a first step, I decided to register for a program at the Seminar Lipschitz Teachers' College, from which, upon graduation, I would receive a diploma and a job. Since I had been left without funds and with no desire to further burden my father, who by then had left Australia and was on his way to join his sick brother, Moshe, in New York, I submitted a local request for a loan, which was approved.

In September 1949, classes began in full force. They were conducted by a very competent staff headed by Eliyahu Katzenelbogen. Among the staff was one of the leading Talmudic giants and the distinguished author of the Talmudic Encyclopedia, Harav Shlomo Yosef Zevin. I enjoyed his classes so much that I decided to join others at his home for extra sessions in *Gemara*. His lessons took the same organized and well-phrased shape as his publications. At the same time, I joined a *Chavrusa* at the Chevron Yeshiva for some additional intensive study of *Gemara*.

In addition, we were very fortunate to have Haim Tzvi Enoch, one of the founders of the State of Israel and molders of Jewish national-religious education. Enoch, who was the first principal of the

Lipschitz Teacher's Seminary, 1960.

experimental school at Kfar Batia, guided us at the Seminar through
a comprehensive system of teaching methodology.

The Seminar was founded in 1921 by Harav Moshe Ostrovski,
also known as Harav Hameiri, and its first principal was Eliezer Meir
Lipschitz, after whom it was later renamed, Michlelet Lipschitz.
Harav Hameiri, who received his *Semicha* from Harav Avraham
Itzchak Hakohen Kook and from Harav Chaim Berlin, was very
active in yeshiva education and in the Mizrachi movement since its
inception in the *Yishuv*.

The program at Seminar Lipschitz consisted largely of a Torah
education but it also included secular subjects such as math, English
and history. In addition, we had courses in psychology and in the
methodology of teaching, which included giving model lessons under the able guidance of Haim Enoch. Usually, these lessons were
given at first-grade level, with a class of six-year-olds. In those years,
the school was located at 17 Hillel Street, Jerusalem. Gradually it
expanded and in 1996 became a fully recognized academic institute
entitled to grant degrees in numerous disciplines. That same year the
seminar opened a new department which combined religious yeshiva
education and academic learning, and offered a degree of Bachelor

Dr. Eliyahu
Katzenelbogen, 1951.

Haim Tzvi Enoch, *circa* 1950.　　　Harav Shlomo Yosef Zevin, *circa* 1960.

in Education and a Teachers Diploma. The
school has now grown into three campuses,
with the original Hillel Street campus largely
for men and the new one on French Hill
largely for women.

In 1951, I graduated with a teaching diploma. By September, I was assigned my
first teaching job at the Or Hachaim School
in Machane Yehuda, Jerusalem. The eighth
graders with whom I was "blessed" came
from poor to middle class Sephardic families, who were not overly anxious to remain

Harav Hameiri
(Ostrovski), *circa* 1930.

in their seats very long and learn. In fact before the first week was
over, a troublesome student who was asked to report to the guidance
counselor (my future wife), was chased over the desks by the princi-

pal, after refusing to report. Except for this experience, I found that Enoch had, indeed, offered valuable advice, which I learned to apply and create curiosity and interest among the thirty kids in the class. Harav Cohen, the principal was very kind and helpful, so that all in all, I had a good and productive year.

Meanwhile, I proceeded to the next step in my educational pursuits. In 1950, even before graduating from the Seminary, I registered at the Hebrew University, with economics as my preference for a major and Jewish History as a minor. Little did I know that once I began my graduate work upon arrival in the United States, I would switch to Jewish history as my major and Jewish philosophy as a minor. Fortunately, the fee at that time per semester was only about 50 Israeli pounds.

The main courses in economics were given by Don Patinkin, who came from Chicago and who soon became world renowned with the publication of his book, *Money, Interest and Prices*. Patinkin, who had dreamed of *aliyah* early on, made all the necessary preparations and began his career at the University in 1949. Before he joined the faculty, economics was just another course among others in the humanities. But with his arrival, a separate department for economics was established, which soon expanded under Patinkin's leadership into a full grown eight-member faculty. Several graduates of his courses later helped reshape the future of Israeli economics. In 1988, Patinkin was chosen as Dean of the Hebrew University. In addition to my classes with Patinkin, I was also taught by Alfred Bonne, who specialized primarily in the domestic economics of Israel and the Middle East.

For Jewish history, my main courses were given by Itzchak Baer and Chaim Hillel Ben-Sasson. Baer, who made *aliyah* from Germany in 1930, dedicated his life's research to the history of the Jews in Christian Spain during the Middle Ages. In 1938, he published his monumental work on the Inquisition. He was recognized at the time as the most distinguished scholar on Spanish Jewry. Ben Sasson was born in Volozhin where he later studied in its famous *Yeshiva* and was ordained by the *Gadol Hador*, Chaim Ozer Grodzenski. He made *aliyah* in 1934 and was a student of Itzchak Baer at the Hebrew University, where he specialized in the study of the Jewish people in the

Middle Ages. In 1949, the year I registered at the University, he joined the Department of Jewish History. He is well known for his numerous publications, including his participation in the publication of a three-volume study on the History of the Jewish People.

The Hebrew University in Jerusalem opened on Mount Scopus in 1925. Since then, it has expanded in its new campus at Givat Ram, to a student population of over 23,000 and a staff of about 1,000. Meanwhile,

Don Patinkin, 1950.

because of the Jordanian blockade, access to the University on Mt.

Itzchak Baer, 1950.

Scopus was nearly impossible until the Six Day War in 1967, when Jerusalem was finally reunited. Despite subsequent Jordanian willingness to allow classes there during this period, the directors decided to temporarily use other buildings in the city. During the War of Independence, the Jordanians had succeeded in cutting off the Mt. Scopus campus from the rest of Jerusalem. Although there were no classes on Mt. Scopus until 1967, Israel kept a skeleton staff there, and sent maintenance crews through Jordanian lines every two weeks accompanied by U.N. security, while secretly smuggling in tank and heavy cannon parts, which were reassembled on Mt. Scopus. The best known temporary building of the Hebrew University and also the largest among them was *Terra Sancta*, where I had most of my classes, as it was chosen to house the department of humanities. The other departments were scattered in other parts of the city.

After several attempts at solving the problem of a home for the University, the question was finally decided with the participation of the government. A large parcel of land was appropriated and construction began which concluded in 1958 with the new campus being dedicated at Givat Ram.

Most of my courses were given in the afternoon, which made it possible, with some effort, for me to also continue my teaching job at the Or Hachaim School in Machane Yehuda, and still make it on time to Terra Sancta in downtown Jerusalem. In addition to the above classes, I also attended other courses, such as Hebrew phonetics by Garbel, a science course by Samburski, and two language classes, in Latin and French, by Gilboa. Moreover, in order to enhance my knowledge of French, I also took a course in that language at the l'École de France.[5]

Meanwhile in 1953, just as I was getting closer to wrapping up my undergraduate work, I decided to quit studies as well as teaching. Many thoughts crossed my mind, which gave me little peace. Guilt feelings about having left my mother and my young brother behind

---

5. *L. Roth*, The Hebrew University, Its Place in the Modern World (London, 1945); *Herbert Parzen*, The Hebrew University, 1925–1935 *(New York: Ktav, 1974)*.

חיים וייצמן, האוניברסיטה העברית בירושלים: כ"ה שנה (ירושלים, תש"י).

גלבר, יואב, תולדות ההתנדבות. כרך ב', המאבק לצבא עברי (ירושלים: יד יצחק בן צבי).

clouded my vision and future plans. Perhaps during these eight years since the War my father and I did not do enough to get to the bottom of their fate.

My father and the *Rebbe* had, indeed, made great efforts through the Red Cross, and I in Israel, through Yad Vashem, to obtain information about the fate of my mother and brother, unfortunately without success. They may have died a horrible death from starvation or disease in the ghetto or more probably, like most Warsaw Jews, in the death camp of Treblinka – the death of *K'doshim* (Martyrs). May HASHEM avenge their innocent blood and the blood of their 6,000,000 brothers and sisters.

My father had turned pessimistic as early as 1946, while I was still with him in Melbourne, despite the urging of the *Zeide* not to give up hope. Like the *Zeide*, I had persisted in the hope that somehow my mother and younger brother would turn up. But as the years passed without so much as an echo – and it was now eight years since the War – I too began to give up hope for the first time and joined my father in accepting the bitter reality.

In view of the above, I decided to join my friends, and join the army. I remembered clearly: ‏(ויקרא ט"ז- י"ט) לא תעמד על דם רעך‎.

As I think about it today, I am convinced, in retrospect that my decision was right and I am very proud of it.

I joined the signal corps and served it with honor for two and a half years. In the first year and a half, after basic training, I was selected to direct a school of communication engineering for cadets, who upon graduation would be drafted into the army. I had the rank of sergeant and I was responsible for the academic program. In the second half of army service, they transferred me to head a committee in charge of translating army communication manuals of several different countries. This was, indeed, an important chapter in my life. Although at first, I submitted a list of words to the *Vaad Halashon* (the government council on the Hebrew language), eventually my own translation committee in the army set and improvised new Hebrew words, since the government Council needed more time than was acceptable to the army.

Life at 24 took on a whole new meaning and direction. Some six months after enlistment marriage followed. With my dear wife's encouragement, whatever I did not complete in my undergraduate studies, I was later able to complete once I returned to my studies, and before I began my graduate program in the U.S.

While in the army, there were occasionally some humorous moments. One day when we were out for routine practice at the firing range as part of basic training, I recall the following incident: The corporal in charge was explaining how to throw a grenade. Since I am left-handed in many activities, I naturally held the grenade which the corporal gave me, in my left hand. But, he insisted that it must be held in the right hand. We were first ordered to line up and fall to the ground. When we were finally ordered to throw the grenade, I did as he insisted and threw it with the right hand. But instead of the grenade heading forward, it rolled down the row at the feet of my fellow soldiers. Fortunately for all of us, it turned out to be only a dummy.

Another incident, not so amusing, occurred one time at about 11 P.M. during night watch. As I was walking around the camp perimeter with my rifle in hand, I suddenly was alerted by a rustle in the bushes and the sound of footsteps coming from the other side. For a moment I held my breath. I then called for the password, thinking that this was possibly another soldier. Since I got no response, I raised my rifle ready to shoot when suddenly a young Yemenite woman with a harmless basket in her hands, full of berries, appeared.[6]

However, the most important event during the early months of my service was my marriage to Chava Besser.

My first encounter with Chava was, actually before I joined the army, when she came to my school, Or Hachaim, to attend to a problem student as a Preventive Service attendant of the school system. Next, I caught sight of her, some weeks later, on an Egged bus going to Jerusalem, when she suddenly rose from her seat to help a sick passenger. Although marriage was not as yet on my mind, I was certainly very impressed by her quick action. One day I went to visit Leib Kalish in Jerusalem, a relative of mine through the *Rebbe's* first marriage. To my complete surprise, Chava, who was a student at the

---

6. Ted Berkman, *Sabra: The Story of the Men and Women Behind the Guns of Israel* (New York: Harper and Row, 1967).

Chava with her parents shortly before leaving Poland, 1936.

Hebrew University in Jerusalem but whose home was in Tel Aviv, stayed with the Kalish family.[7] As I later discovered, her parents were friends of the family.[8]

Meanwhile, I served in the army and put these encounters with Chava to rest for the time being. A few months passed. Then one *Shabbos* morning while on leave, after prayer by my uncle Shmuel Ele, the *Rebbe* at the time, in Tel-Aviv, I was approached by Yakir Yud, a close friend of the family, who proposed to arrange a match between Chava and me.

So it all began. As soon as the months of basic training were over, I was able to leave camp almost daily after hours, and go out on dates with Chava. Some six months into army service, we got engaged. Preparations were under way and within four months, on August 31, 1953, the great event – our marriage – was celebrated. The hall known as "Ulamey Ruth," Tel Aviv, was packed with close to a

7. See Appendix.

8. See Appendix.

A photo of me in the Israeli army, 1954.

thousand guests in attendance, with my uncle, the *Rebbe*, being the *mesader chuppah* and *kiddushin*. It was a beautiful *simcha* and, indeed, a match made in heaven.

Unfortunately, my father, whose brother Moshe was very ill, could not make it to Israel to attend. My in-laws, Yehuda Arie Leib and Devorah Besser, who originally also came from Otwock in 1936,

Author's Wedding, August 31, 1953.

were a very fine couple. They lived very close to us, and did their best to make our first steps in married life easier, especially during my army service. Their son Moshe, Chava's brother, later married Sarah, the Gerrer *Rebbe's* granddaughter. My father-in-law, who was a devoted *chossid* of the *Rebbe*, became even more attached after Moshe's marriage. Together, my in-laws ran a fruit and vegetable store on Ben Yehudah Street which was very close to the major hotels. They provided these hotels with most of their produce. It was really my mother-in-law who was the business woman. Often, she would bring bag-loads of fruit and vegetables to her son and daughter-in-law, climbing many steps in the process. My in-laws would be frequent visitors to us and our one-year-old baby Malka. Several

The Besser family, 1946.

years later, after we had settled in the States, they came to see us and our three children whom they loved dearly. Chava's brother Moshe, a great Talmudic genius, studied for many years in the famous Poneviezh *Yeshiva* of B'nei B'rak.

Thus began our 62-year marriage bond, which was, unfortunately, interrupted on October 19, 2015, when my dearest and most precious was laid to rest in Jerusalem. These years with Chava were our golden years, and her absence has left a deep void in my life.

Shortly after our marriage, Chava introduced me to her Tel Aviv social circle of friends who often met at each other's homes. The women would meet every Friday in a local café. This affluent circle of men and their spouses, mostly professionals and businessmen, was unique and indeed a cross-section of the modern, Orthodox Jewish community in Israel. Many of them served together during the War of Independence in the Ben Shemen region.

They included the following: Avram Pressler, the Israeli representative on the German Reparations Commission; Shaya Prives, lawyer; Yoshe Goldfinger, the biggest diamond dealer in Israel; David Kinek, engineer; Israel Mintzer, owner of a book store; Israel Erlich, representative of the Jewish Agency in Rome, later director of the Tel Aviv Burial Society and author of several books in Judaica;

Arie and Devorah Besser,
Chava's parents, 1953.

Shmuel Strubinski, manufacturer; Yaakov Be'eri, an engineer; David Fridman, director of Bank Leumi, Haim Basok, a lawyer, Tzvi Redlich, manager at El Al and Reuven Segal, a well-known building contractor. Except for most of the wives, none of the above are still alive.

In addition, my friends from that group and their wives who are still living are Alter Velner, editor of the daily *Hatzofeh*, later director of the *Itim* news agency and author of several books in Judaica, Yosef Frumer, owner of a hardware store, Benjamin Epstein, teacher, Menachem Lebel, school supervisor, and Yosl Cederbaum, a businessman.

Shortly after our wedding, we moved into a small but lovely apartment on Amram Gaon Street, Tel Aviv, which my in-laws purchased for us. A few months before my discharge, Malka, our first child, named after my mother, was born; she was our only

child born in Israel. Her arrival, followed in later years by our other two children, Varda and Aaron Dovid, brought great joy to our lives. Malka is now a grandmother and a business woman running a Wall Street consulting company and married to Allan Treuhaft, a C.P.A; Varda, also a grandmother and physical therapist, is married to Bernie Neuhaus, a trader in aluminum; and Aaron Dovid, a Rebbi, married to Tamar, a business manager.

To assure a decent livelihood, both of us went to work. Chava became the superintendent of several kindergartens, and I taught until the early afternoon. In the evenings, I became the assistant night editor of the daily, *Haboker*, under the very capable leadership of its editor, Yaakov Gruman. Chava's workload at the kindergartens and mine at the school came to six days a week. At *Haboker*, my job was four days a week from 7pm until midnight. My responsibility at the newspaper was to select and draft the foreign news reports for the front page. This was based primarily on cables dispatched by our own correspondents overseas and the tele printer reports from the news agencies Reuters, Associated Press, United Press, and the French News Agency, as well as earlier reports that had been kept in our archives. Chava, who took courses in supervision at Hebrew University, was very efficient in running and supervising her kindergartens. My work at *Haboker* was, indeed, quite a challenge and extremely fascinating, but as is the case with most newspapers, had its surprises, and also suffered eventual demise.

One night we received word from the news agencies that Chaim Weizmann, the first president of Israel, had passed away. So we all got to work and drafted an appropriate and extensive report as well as what was our standard policy, a headline. However, at the last minute before the paper went to press, we received word, to our

May, 1965. (*HaBoker Daily Newspaper*)

surprise, that Weizmann was still very much alive. He died several
days later. On another occasion, also just before we went to press,
we found a gap on page one that had to be filled. An advertisement
for a bookstore was quickly found in the commercial archives which
perfectly fit the gap. The following *Shabbos* I met my friend Israel

Mintzer who owned that store. He expressed surprise to see the ad: "I haven't advertised in the *Haboker* for over a year," he declared.

Two years after I got the job, along with many others, I was fired as part of *Haboker's* plan to sharply cut the staff. I was among the last to be hired. Therefore, I was among the first to be fired. The paper, like many others in Israel and around the world, had been suffering from a sharp drop in readership. I was invited some two months later to return, despite the compensation that I had been paid. Shortly after that, *Haboker* went out of business.

Now that I was left with only my teaching job, which meant a sharply reduced income, my thoughts quickly shifted to the possibility of visiting my father in the U.S. Although we were frequently on the phone (letters were no longer the way to communicate), I had not seen him since 1949. The summer was about to begin and I would be free to go. It was May 1957, several months after the Sinai War, better known as Operation Kadesh. Three countries: Israel, Great Britain, and France went to war against Egypt after Abdul Nasser, the dictator, nationalized the Suez Canal and blocked Israeli shipping from passing through the Canal or reaching Eilat. So once Chava and I agreed on the trip, I left for the States. On the way I made a short stop-over by our cousins Meir and Sola Perel, who lived in the university town of Louvain, Belgium.

When I left Israel, it did not even dawn on me that it was the beginning of a new chapter and a major change in our lives. First I landed in Naples, Italy, where I boarded a train for Rome. In Rome I planned to obtain a French transit visa, which was then necessary to cross into Belgium. So upon arrival in Rome, I headed for the French consulate in the city. At the consulate, I approached an official to explain the purpose of my visit. He roughly interrupted me by ordering me to remove my hat. He then advised me to go back to Tèl Aviv for the French visa. Realizing that this encounter will come to no good, I left the consulate without further delay. Since I had to go north anyway, I boarded a train for Venice in the hope of a better and less offensive reception at the small French consulate there. Indeed, I was right. The consulate was on the third floor. I climbed up the steep steps, and entered the office where I was greeted kindly by the consul himself, who was quite relaxed and without customers.

Within a matter of minutes, I was back on the streets of Venice on my way to the train station. The Consul himself filled out my application and stamped the necessary transit visa into my passport.

The trip to Belgium was very scenic and picturesque. After winding its way through the steep, snow-covered mountains of the Italian and French Alps, the train headed for Paris, where I arrived some ten hours later, at the Gare de Lyon station.

From Paris it took about an hour to reach Louvain. My cousins greeted me graciously and there was excitement in the air as we met. Meir and Sola Perel, both survivors, passed away several years ago, leaving behind two children Esther and Leon. They were a lovely and extremely charming couple who owned several clothing stores in Louvain, the university town, as well as in several other places. Sola, whose maiden name was Ferleiger, was a first cousin of Arie Besser, my father-in-law. The conversation in their store was in French, which helped me polish my limited knowledge of the language. Meir took me around the country, including Brussels, the capital. Moreover, they made sure that I feel at home during my visit, and I stayed with them some two weeks.

Finally, I prepared myself to complete the trip to the United States. I expressed my appreciation for the warm reception. Meir drove me to Paris, where we said goodbye to each other. In Paris I took a train to the port town of Dieppe where I arrived, after a two hour ride, ready to board the ship. Since I had a British passport, my plan was to first head to Montreal, from where I would continue to the States, after obtaining a visitor's visa. I had not yet had a visa for the States, which in those days was required.

In the meantime, while the security man examined my passport, the service crew forwarded my luggage to the ship.

Although everything seemed to be O.K., I was in for a surprise. The French security man, who clearly failed to comprehend my status and knew nothing of my past, charged: "You were born in Poland, you are an Australian citizen and British subject, but live in Israel and you are headed for Canada?"

He refused to allow me on board, and ordered my luggage returned. He told me that if I wanted to go to Canada, I should return to Paris and also purchase a return ticket to Israel. In other words,

RMS *Queen Elizabeth, which I took to New York, 1957.*

he wanted to make sure that after the visit to Canada I would leave the country. Since the next boat was docking in New York, I would at least, also need a U.S. transit visa. He, of course, did not know that my plan was to get to the U.S. In the end, they unloaded my luggage, and the next train took me back to Paris. This was, indeed, some adventure! Once I was back in the capital, I placed my luggage in a locker at the station and headed straight for the Lloyd's shipping office.

Now began the hassle. At Lloyd's, I was informed that despite my British passport, I first had to go and get a Canadian visa. When I reached the Canadian consulate, there was a long line of people stretching for several blocks, probably anxious to settle in Canada after the War. In my desperation, and in order not to miss the next boat that was due to depart that same evening from Cherbourg for New York, I rushed for the door and somehow made it in. But here too, to my dismay, they refused to grant me the visa unless I first got a U.S. transit visa. However, they did promise a visa immediately once I got back with the American transit visa. So out I hurried to the U.S. consulate which was not far, but was about to close for a two-hour lunch break. Thank G-d I made it, was promised the transit visa but got it only after their lunch break, returned to the Canadians, got their visa, and headed back to Lloyd's for the return ticket. By three in the afternoon, I was on the train for the two-hour ride to Cherbourg and finally got on the boat. All is well that ends well.

These were the days when travel by air was not yet very common. The ship, none other than the luxury liner, *Queen Elizabeth*, was scheduled that evening to depart for New York by 7.00 P.M.

The story had a happy ending. They gave me a cabin with four beds and the purser told me that since three beds were vacant, I could use any bed I chose. In the end, I had the cabin all to myself. Four and a half days later, on June 11, 1957, we finally ended our trip across the Atlantic and docked in New York harbor.

Chapter VI

The U.S.A.

ALTHOUGH THIS WAS TO HAVE BEEN a short visit to see my father and the rest of the family, uncles and aunts who were children of the *Rebbe*, I ended up staying in America for almost 60 years. This was thus the beginning of the main chapter in my life. I joined my father at his home in Forest Hills. We spent one day together, as I was on a three day transit visa only, and on the advice of my lawyer, I left immediately for Ottawa, Canada. In Ottawa, I headed for the U.S. consulate, where I was able to have the transit visa replaced with a four-year visitor's visa, with which I then returned to New York.

Back at home with my father, we discussed and weighed the various options for me to consider. After consulting with my wife, Chava, I took up the suggestion that most appealed to me at that time, and began to look for a teaching position. Within a few days, my lawyer was able to get me a work permit and I headed for the job market. A week later, I was on my way, along with four other candidates, to the Yeshiva of North Plainfield, New Jersey, where there was an opening in the field. I was interviewed like all the others, and was immediately offered the job.

As we were returning in the van to New York, I recall one candidate making a poignant observation: "When I seek a job in some of the *yeshivas* in New York, they find my beard too short, but when I come to Plainfield, it is too long!"

My father with Efroim Rosen and Chaskel Taub

Gradually, the idea that I was here to stay, at least for a while, and make some money after the setback in Tel Aviv, began to sink in. Although I was delighted to be with my father once again, my youthful idealism began to falter in face of the unhappy reality with growing family responsibilities.

I was soon able to supplement my *yeshiva* job with an afternoon teaching position, three times a week in a Hillside, New Jersey, Talmud Torah. At this point in time, my wife, Chava and daughter, Malka were still in Tel Aviv, and I had not yet found a permanent residence in New York for all of us. So, to meet my schedule in both places, I rented a place in North Plainfield. Moreover, I also took driving lessons, and for the first time in my life, I became a car owner of a used De Soto, with which I hit the road. Thus I got myself fully prepared for the school year.

Meanwhile, Chava began preparations later that year, to join me in the States. The change was not an easy one as it involved separation from her parents, her work in the kindergartens and saying goodbye to relatives, friends and country. Before she left, our apartment in Tel Aviv was rented out and during our absence, its good care was entrusted to my in-laws. Finally, in the following year, on June 18,

Rav Avraham Wyszkowski,
my father

1958, at the beginning of the summer, Chava and Malka arrived in New York. By that time, I had already finished the school year in Plainfield, and decided to quit both New Jersey schools in favor of New York. At about that time, I was hired at Robert Gordis Day School in Belle Harbor, Queens, as well as at Marine Park Talmud Torah (Brooklyn), in the afternoons.

Before Chava's arrival, I also found a nice, comfortable apartment at 712 Crown Street, Crown Heights, Brooklyn. I chose this apartment because most of our family lived in the area. Besides, the neighborhood had a good selection of *yeshivas*, and was not too far from my new places of work. Shortly after her arrival, Chava was hired as a seventh-grade teacher in the Yeshiva of Crown Heights, under the capable leadership of Rabbi Joseph M. Baumol. The school, which was on the same street as our apartment and only a 15 minute walk, was also quite suitable for our daughter Malka. Three years later we registered her at Yeshiva of Crown Heights from where she eventually graduated.

By the end of that summer, another important and happy event, in my life, took place. My dear father, who had suffered for many years of his early life from anxiety and distress because of my mother, Malka and brother, Yisroel, at last re-married. The marriage to Esther Jaroslowicz, conducted by Rabbi Mordechai Twersky, who was the *mesader chuppah* and *kiddushin*, took place on August 31, 1958. After they got married, my father moved into Esther's apartment on Mosholu Parkway, in the Bronx.

Gradually, we got to know Esther, and although she could never replace my dear mother, Malka, *a"h*, we got along just fine. Moreover, we found her to be a very fine and warm person, fond of, and devoted to, my father and his welfare. All in all they turned out to be a fine couple. Although she had no children of her own, over the years, she became closely attached to our Malka, and later to our other children Varda, and Aaron Dovid, as well.

Thus, we got ourselves settled into our new American environment at the youthful ages of 28 (Chava) and 29 (me). For us this was a major social and, to some extent, also linguistic change, from Hebrew to English, although at home Hebrew continued to prevail. I had gone through several such changes in the past. When I came to Australia at the age of twelve, I spoke Yiddish, but soon learned to speak English. Eight years later, upon my arrival in Israel, it was Hebrew and now in the U.S., it was back to English again. On the other hand, for Chava and Malka, English was definitely a challenge. As for myself, thank G-d, language adjustment, was rather quick without any visible accent problems.

Ten years after leaving Australia, my father was re-married, and he too gradually learned to accept his new reality. Marriage to Esther helped him heal the wounds and focus more favorably on the future.

Avraham and Esther Wyszkowski

He became a successful businessman, first in nursing homes and later, in diamonds as well. At the same time, he joined the Young Israel Shul of Rabbi Zevulun Charlap, which was next door, and only a block away from Montefiore Hospital. Rabbi Charlap, on the faculty of Yitzchak Elchonon (Yeshiva University), was a very respectable and gracious person. He invited my father to speak occasionally on *Shabbos* and give a *Gemara* class for young doctors from Montefiore.

Thank G-d for *Shabbos*, which often distracted him from his daily problems. That was the day to spend more time with Torah study and with family. We also used to make our rounds and visit uncles, aunts, cousins, and friends who lived, for the most part in close proximity in those early years, in Crown Heights. They reciprocated with frequent visits to us.

At the same time, we thought Sunday to be the best time for a visit to my father and Esther, since they lived on Mosholu Parkway, a beautiful section of the Bronx, but for us, some distance away. During those visits, my father never even once spoke of my mother and brother, or of anything pertaining to the past. Our visits to them were usually accompanied by a lavish dinner ably prepared by Esther. Often we would find my father outside in a chair on the grassy Mosholu Parkway deeply engrossed in a *Gemara* page.

As for prayer on *Shabbos*, the entire family used to gather in our own Shul on President Street near Schenectady Avenue, Crown Heights, where we all lived. The place was under the good care of my aunt, Rachel Taub, who lived upstairs. She was the mother of *Rav* Yisroel Dovid Taub, who later opened his own Shul in Flatbush. She was a very warm and gracious woman; she never remarried after the early passing of her husband, Chaskel, my mother's older brother, in the 1950s.

Among the new friends that we made in the States were Avram and Sarah Raphaeli, a young couple with deep roots in Israel and with whom we struck an enduring and especially close relationship. Both they and their children found their match. Often we would spend time together, whether at home, in Long Beach bungalows during the summer, at the beach and park, or at the annual Israeli parade in Manhattan. One day Avram accepted a principal's job in far-away Atlanta, Georgia (an offer which I had been advised earlier to turn down). They eventually moved to that city, where they remained for about three years but always stayed in constant touch with us.

That same year, they concluded that it was time for them to return to Israel, since in those days Atlanta offered few prospects of a proper Jewish environment for their children. This, in fact, was the reason for my earlier rejection. Upon their return, Avram was appointed principal of the Lipschitz Teachers Seminar from which I had graduated, and Sarah joined *Michlala*, an excellent seminary for girls, both in Jerusalem.

On September 12, 1960, two years after we took up residence

in Crown Heights, Chava gave birth to our second daughter. On that same day, which was to have been the first day of school, New York was hit by a powerful storm, Hurricane Donna. Dr. Solomon, Chava's physician, driving his own car, rushed her to the hospital. Although Donna would perhaps have been a good choice, instead, we named our daughter Varda, after her great grandmother. As for myself, I was stranded in Belle Harbor where I worked because of the storm. Conditions were so bad that the salty Bay waters reached the handles of my car doors. Eventually, I was transferred across the Marine Park Bridge by an army truck. Varda has since grown up and is a great mother and grandmother as well as a successful physical therapist.

During 1961–1963, we rented bungalows for the summer, and joined our uncles and aunts, including Avram and Tzipora Shenker; Efroim and Sara Rosen; Yitzchok and Yona Taub; Yisroel and Edith Taub; and Dovid and Rivka Taub. The first year we went to Lake Mohegan in Upstate New York, where the weather was great, except for the mosquitos. I recall Yisroel and Edith, *a"h*, as they arrived. He never left the air-conditioned car, and instead invited us to join him inside.

The following summer we switched to Long Beach. In all of these places the kids had a great time and the movie cameras always kept rolling. We were joined, in those early years, by the Raphaeli family, who were a wonderful couple and with whom we had much in common.

Beginning with the summer of 1963, we joined the teaching faculty at Camp Yavneh, in the scenic countryside of Northwood, New Hampshire. My wife taught Hebrew and I Jewish History, four days a week between 9 A.M. and 12 noon. The campers taking the courses were students from the Prozdor High School in Boston, which was under the direction of a scholarly friend, Dr. Jacques K. Mikliszanski. Many of these students later entered Hebrew Teacher's College of Newton headed by Dean Eisig Zilbershlag. Several courses, including mine, were for credit, and whoever earned it, was exempt from taking those same courses during the year at the Prozdor High School. Classes were generally conducted outside and in the shade.

Camp Yavneh

Moshe Avital and his charming wife, Chana, were in charge of the camp, and under their leadership, the Hebrew language was given high priority. We made many friends at this camp, among them, Baruch Rappaport, who was also with me on the teaching staff in Belle Harbor; Sara Reguer, who, for many years, has been director of the Department for Judaic Studies at Brooklyn College; Yeshaya Kronman, who was my colleague at Yeshiva of Flatbush, where he was Chairman of the Department of Jewish philosophy and who now lives in retirement in Jerusalem, and Ben Zion and Chana Melamed, who later returned to Israel where Chana was appointed International Director of Emunah Women. For the next five years, Camp Yavneh, in the woods of New Hampshire, was where we spent our summer months.

During the Yavneh period, our daughters Malka and Varda were together with us. Malka, who had become a teenager, spent the last two summers at Camp Naara in the Catskill Mountains.

Faculty in Yavneh

Meanwhile, on June 5, 1967, the Six Day War broke out between Israel and its Arab neighbors, Egypt, Jordan, and Syria. Israel swept across the Sinai Desert and Judea and Samaria, including East Jerusalem and the Kotel, all in six days. Although over 600 Jewish lives were lost, it was a historic victory for Israel. Aside from the land seized, in the first day of the war, Israel's brave pilots destroyed the entire Egyptian air force.

As soon as camp was over, we flew to Israel, the second trip since we left the country in 1957. Indeed we found that much had changed in ten years.

Meanwhile, as the years went by, reality was gaining the upper hand in shaping our lives. In the early years since our arrival in the States we kept the suitcase ready, so to speak, for a return to Israel. The presence of my father and most of my family, however, as well as the daily American lifestyle, including financial security, weighed heavily in favor of staying where we were.

After our return from our trip to Israel in August 1967, we

decided to leave Crown Heights and rent an apartment in Flatlands, Brooklyn. After a few inquiries, we found a suitable place at 1039 East 57 St., in the two family home owned by the charming Bronner family. At first when we settled in Crown Heights, the neighborhood was very congenial. Most of our family and some friends we had known from Israel lived there. But demographically, Crown Heights began to change and so did the social environment. Additionally, the area was no longer as peaceful and safe as it had been in the past, and some of our family members already began to move else-where. What especially shook us up upon returning from Israel that summer was an incident that took place right before our eyes. Our apartment was on the ground floor facing the street. One night past midnight, a young couple who may have lived in the same building, started an altercation in front of our windows. The brawl got noisier and more heated from minute to minute, until suddenly we heard the crack of gunfire. I do not know how the affair ended, since we instantly stepped away from the shades through which we peeped. The incident convinced us that it was time for us to move as well, as the area was no longer sufficiently secure.

The years we lived with the Bronner family, from 1967 until 1973, were very pleasant and happy ones. Shortly after we moved, several events and changes took place in our family. In 1968, our daughter Malka graduated from the Yeshiva of Crown Heights and began Central High School for girls of Yeshiva University which she completed in 1973.

The following year, on February 14, 1969, Aaron Dovid, our third child was born. We were all happy and excited to welcome a son after two daughters. Our son grew up to become a Ben Torah, very bright and serious, and is learning in the Yeshiva of Chaim Berlin. Jewish education and promotion of Torah life as a Rebbi in the classroom was his ambition. He is happily married to Tamar Mordowitz, his dear wife, and has seven lovely children.

That same year, I returned to my academic studies for a B.A. at Yeshiva University, which I had left unfinished in the 1950s at the Hebrew University in Jerusalem, completing all requirements for the degree. I then began the long road at Bernard Revel Graduate School towards my M.A. and eventually also a Ph.D. degree.

In June 1970, my
Masters project: "Jews
in Crime in New York
City, 1895–1899," was
approved by the faculty
of Bernard Revel Grad-
uate School of Yeshiva
University.[1] A letter of
confirmation was signed
by Dr. Sidney B. Hoenig,
chairman of the faculty

Yeshiva University

executive committee. This study was a forerunner of a later doctoral
thesis research, advanced by another student and based on two more
similar Masters projects on Jews in crime. Finally, on January 31,
1979, I successfully completed my doctoral thesis under the title:
"A Community in Conflict (American Jewry during the Great European Immigration)." This study was also approved by the Faculty
of Bernard Revel Graduate School, following my successful Oral
Defense.[2] A letter to this effect was signed by Sid Z. Leiman, Dean
of the School. The thesis was published in 1991, by the University
Press of America under the above title.[3]

At about that time, a change also took place in my place of work.
During a casual visit to a friend at Yeshiva of Flatbush High School,
academically one of the best Jewish high schools in America, I was
asked to meet the principal, David Eliach, who then invited me to
join the faculty. It was already June, almost the end of the school
year, and with eleven years of teaching in the Belle Harbor yeshiva
behind me, I questioned the wisdom of such a step. Not wishing to
give up on me, Eliach assured me that with my permission, he would
arrange such a transfer with the Belle Harbor administrator.

In the end, his efforts were successful. I was, thereupon, appointed

---

1. See Appendix for Masters approval letter.

2. See Appendix, Yeshiva University letter of approval for Ph.D.

3. Wyszkowski, *A Community in Conflict*; Aaron Rothkoff, *Bernard Revel: Builder of
American Jewish Orthodoxy* (Philadelphia: JPS, 1972); Gilbert Klaperman, *The Story of
Yeshiva University* (Toronto: Macmillan, 1969).

Author's Doctoral graduation, Yeshiva University, 1979.

chairman of the Jewish history department and began in September 1970. The Yeshiva of Flatbush consists of elementary and high school divisions. The entire Judaic Studies program is taught in modern Hebrew, and about half of some 150 graduates learn for at least a year in Israel, in a *yeshiva* for boys and in a seminary for girls. Furthermore, upon their return to the States, most of them are admitted to the best universities in the country.

Meanwhile, the apartment in which we lived at the Bronners was modern, large and indeed very comfortable and pleasant. Two amusing incidents that took place while we were there are not easily forgotten. One morning, a Jewish neighbor came out in tears, dressed in black. When asked about it, she offered the following:" I was hit with two tragedies in one day. First my mother died, but she was an old woman. Now, my dog also died! That's just too much." On

Yeshiva of Flatbush Joel Braverman High School

another occasion on a nice summer day, a group of women, neighbors of ours, who were sitting and relaxing outside, were engaged in conversation. While they were chatting, a moving van drove up to another house down the block, and began bringing out furniture. One of the women who saw this at some distance observed: "The furniture looks just like mine." Soon the movers finished their job and drove off. When the woman was done talking to her friends she walked over to her house only to find that all her furniture was gone.

Meanwhile, because of the growth of my family to five members, it became necessary to consider the possibility of buying a house. Although, living with the Bronners was extremely comfortable and pleasant – a strong reason for not rushing to get out – the growing need for our own house was clear. Just a few hundred yards from where we lived and on the same street, an Italian contractor had built a block of some twelve houses. In January 1973, we made our move and went to contract. Several months later we finally moved into the three-apartment dwelling at 1274 East 57 Street. This was our first piece of property in this country. Two of the three apartments we soon rented out, one on the second floor and the other, a basement apartment. Becoming a landlord was not exactly a pleasure, but we generally got along well with our tenants, one of whom was a young

Teaching at Yeshiva of Flatbush

lawyer who lived in the basement apartment. He was single, very sociable and worked to the late hours of the night. During 1967–1983, when we lived in Flatlands, first at the Bronners and then in our own house on East 57 St., we became members of the Young Israel of Flatlands.

In 1976, the first marriage in our family took place. Malka, our oldest daughter, married Allan Treuhaft, from a lovely family in Cleveland. This brought us great joy, and my dear Chava began what she loved most – shopping. She was a frequent visitor to the department stores of Brooklyn and Manhattan, always determined to have our children as well as herself dressed in the best and the latest style. The wedding was celebrated at Terrace on the Park, in Queens.

After Yeshiva of Crown Heights moved its facilities to the Flatlands area in 1974, Chava left the school and transferred to the Sephardic Yeshiva of Magen David. In 1981 however, she joined me in the high school of Yeshiva of Flatbush where she was appointed school librarian, a position she held for 14 years. A growing problem she encountered upon her arrival in the library was the large number of books that were never returned, and often lost forever. She immediately took steps to correct the system and prevent such problems

Wedding of our eldest daughter Malka to Allan Treuhaft, 1976.

in the future. There were also many rare books, which were moved
to a safer and better place in the school. Chava undoubtedly left her
mark on the library.

Meanwhile, Aaron Dovid turned six in 1975, and began his education, for the most part, in Yeshiva Toras Emes, Boro Park, from which
he eventually graduated 12 years later. He then spent two years in
Kerem Be-Yavneh, Israel, after which he returned to the States and
entered Yeshiva Chaim Berlin. My daughter Varda attended Crown
Heights Yeshiva for her elementary education starting in the year
1966, and continued high school at Central of Yeshiva University.
Malka, my oldest, graduated Central High School in 1973. Whereas
both Malka and Varda continued their academic studies at Brooklyn
College, Varda pursued a medical career and later also graduated
from SUNY Downstate Medical Center as a physical therapist. In
1981, an important wedding took place.

Varda, my younger daughter, married Bernard Neuhaus, of a well-
known family in Washington Heights, New York. Their wedding
also took place in Terrace on the Park.

Malka entered the business world, and after a short period at

Malka and
Allan Treuhaft,
1976.

various firms, including Met Life, opened her own Wall Street consulting company.

Beginning in 1979, and for the next five years, we were all hit with
a succession of bad news, most of it coming from Israel. In that year,
Moshe Besser, Chava's brother in Israel, was diagnosed with mela-
noma and within a few months he passed away at the young age of
38. He had been a great *talmid chochom* and after undergoing a series
of tests by the Chief Rabbi, Shlomo Goren, he was scheduled for an
appointment as a Dayan (equivalent to a judge). He left behind his
wife, Sarah, and their five lovely daughters, who by now are happily
married with children and grandchildren of their own.

Arie, my father-in-law, passed away soon afterward in the year
1980 at the age of 70 due to incredible grief for the great loss of his

Moshe Besser at his Wedding

Varda and Bernard Neuhaus

son. He had come to Israel from Poland in 1936, with Devorah, my mother-in-law. He was dedicated to his family and was a faithful follower of the Chassidic dynasty of the Gerrer *Rebbe*.

The following year, my father Avraham, who had together with me wandered from country to country after our escape from the Nazi beasts, passed away in New York at the age of 71. He had been ill for two years, but never stopped delivering speeches, occasional sermons at family *simchas*, and his *Gemara* series to the doctors from Montefiore Hospital. I later published many of his presentations under the title משכן אברהם.

Three years later, Devorah, my mother-in-law who had turned 74, passed away after a lengthy struggle with cancer. She too suffered much grief upon the passing of her son Moshe. She had come to the States and stayed with us while undergoing treatment, but shortly

Sarah Besser and her daughters

after her return to Israel, she lost her struggle. All her life she was a fighter, truly dedicated to her children whom she loved very much.

That same year, 1984, my uncle, the *Rebbe*, *Rav* Shmuel-Eliyahu Taub, passed away in Tel Aviv where he had lived most of his life, and was buried on Har Hazesim. He was not only a great *Rebbe* but also a person full of charm and warmth, ready to greet every man with open arms. Like his father, he composed several hundred *nigunim*. He was succeeded as the new Modzitzer *Rebbe* by *Rav* Yisroel Dan, his son. Harav Dan finally made the move and transferred Beit Modzitz to B'nei B'rak, where it is presently a great center for Torah and *neginah*.

In 1983, we made a major change which left its mark and had a positive effect in our daily lives. We sold our house at 1274 East 57 Street and moved to Flatbush. During our residence in Flatlands, we continued to drive our children to schools in Flatbush and Boro Park, daily. Flatlands, however, had changed very little during the sixteen years of our residence. The Jewish environment remained stagnant, and few Jews moved into the area.

We therefore decided to make the move and buy a house in

Matzeivah of my father,
Har Hamenuchos, 1981.

Flatbush. It is now some 34 years since my wife Chava and I began enjoying this neighborhood on East 10th Street, during the prime of our lives. It is also the place where my son Aaron Dovid grew up, and got married. Although all of our children, thank G-d, are now happily married with children of their own, most of whom are also married, the nostalgic connection remains strong. Our children, grandchildren and great grandchildren attended – and some still do – the best *yeshivas*, with great prospects for a bright future in Torah and professional life.

The house I live in is only minutes away from *shuls*, schools, book-stores, and kosher supermarkets. On *Shabbos* we *davened* at Congregation Shaarei Torah on East 12 St., headed by *Rav* Hillel David, and for *Yom Tovim* at Congregation Ishei Yisroel of Modzitz on East 7 St., headed by my cousin *Rav* Yisroel Dovid Taub. Over the last two decades, *Rav* Taub has been engaged in a monumental enterprise, publishing several important manuscripts of *Divrei Torah*, including the famous *Hagodah* of the *Rebbe*, my *Zeide*, Shaul Yedidya Elozor and his father, as well as of the Kuzimer *Rebbe*, the founder of Modzitz. These works include:[4] ישא ברכה, דברי ישראל, הגדה של פסח, ויד יחזקאל.

On weekdays I chose to go to Congregation Kehal Veretsky on Ave. L, headed by *Rav* Landau. Within a short time, moreover, I was able to join some learning groups including the Daf Yomi.

Meanwhile, in 1980, I was appointed adjunct professor at Brooklyn College, where, in addition to Jewish History, I also inaugurated a course in the Yiddish language, for the first time at the College. The department chairman was Samuel Abramsen. In recognition of this course, the College also agreed to grant full accreditation for a similar course that I gave as an elective to seniors at the Yeshiva of Flatbush High School. In 1985, I left the College in favor of New York University, after I was invited to give a similar course there. Aside from my obligations at Flatbush High School and NYU, towards the end of the 1980s, I was appointed evaluator for credit, in Yiddish and Hebrew, at Empire State College. The college students would visit me at home, where I would make the evaluation. The credits awarded by me would range from 3 to 16 for each evaluation. My relationship with this College lasted for over 20 years. In addition, I have been invited from time to time for lecture presentations in Jewish history by colleges, schools, associations, and societies.

From 1988 to 1993, we signed up for a three-week summer seminar in Jerusalem sponsored by the World Zionist Organization-Department for Religious Jewish Education in the Diaspora. The seminar was held at the five-star Renaissance Hotel, under the able direction of Dr. Prell. The courses, which were extremely interesting, were presented by a very select panel, which included the popular Torah commentator Nehama Leibowitz and the founder of the Michlala Seminar for girls, Yehudah Kupperman.

In 1999, we celebrated a great Simcha. Aaron Dovid Wyszkowski,

---

4. שאול ידידיה אלעזר זצוק"ל, ישא ברכה, נערך ונסדר ע"י נכדו הרב ישראל דוד, ניו יורק, תשע"ג: ישראל זצוק"ל, דברי ישראל, נערך ונסדר ע"י הרב ישראל דוד, ניו יורק, תשע"ו: יחזקאל מקוזמיר זצוק"ל ושמואל אליהו מזוואליןזצוק"ל, יד יחזקאל, נערך ונסדר ע"י הרב ישראל דוד, ניו יורק, תשע"ב.

the youngest of our children, was married to Tamar Mordowitz of a large and well known family in Monsey, New York. This was indeed a beautiful and joyous wedding for all of us, which was celebrated at the Atrium in Monsey. Aaron Dovid and Tamar are now happily married, living with their children in Brooklyn.

The year 2002, marked a turning point in my life. That was the year I reached the age of 73 and decided to retire from Yeshiva of Flatbush High School. Earlier that year, on April 4th, *b"h*, I successfully underwent cardiac bypass surgery. After having worked there for 32 years, which in Hebrew is numerically equal to the word Lev (heart), G-d must have given me a signal. I also gave up my teaching position at NYU, and some five years later, in 2007, I retired from Empire State College. Two years later, we bought a condo apartment in Century Village, Deerfield Beach, Florida.

Now that both of us were retired, it was possible to spend a few months each winter at the Village. The Jewish Orthodox community in Century Village built a large and beautiful Young Israel, which now numbers over a thousand members. It is a very active and socially friendly group consisting of modern Orthodox, Orthodox and *Chassidim*, primarily *Ashkenazim*, but also a sizable number of *Sephardim*. There are numerous study programs, such as *Daf Yomi*, with an average attendance of over 60 people, as well as general subjects like Hebrew language, Torah and *Tania*.

The *Shabbos* program which is especially intensive includes the eloquent sermons of *Rav* Yisroel Eidelman, the *Mara D'asra*, and afternoon lectures, usually with hundreds in attendance. Over the past thirteen years, I have been an active participant in this series, presenting, annually, a lecture in Jewish history.

In 2006, *Rav* Yisroel Dan Taub *zt"l* the Modzitzer *Rebbe*, passed away after an extended illness. He left behind *Rebbetzin* Rachel who is the mother of today's *rebbe*, *Rav* Chaim Shaul Taub. In 2009, Esther, my dear stepmother, also gave way to an extended illness. She had suffered from Alzheimer's disease for several years. Esther had been a devoted wife to my father throughout their marriage. She was also very close with us and our children.

Aaron Dovid and Tamar Wyszkowski, 1999.

Chapter VII

The World Through Adventure

EVER SINCE we had settled in the States, both Chava and I loved to travel and see the world we live in. At first most of our trips were to Israel and we took our kids with us whenever it was possible. As they grew up, we began to expand our geographical zone, to include various European countries. Switzerland, which we visited several times, topped the list.

The following pages offer a selection of some of the trips to Israel, European countries, and a variety of places in the United States and Canada. Between 1957, when I first left Israel, and 1975, we made frequent trips to Israel during the summer, primarily to visit parents and to spend some of our vacation time there. Our friends always greeted us warmly, and were delighted to meet with us and spend time together.

Our first European trip was in 1976, when we took our kids, Varda and Aaron Dovid, to France, Belgium, Holland, Switzerland, and then back to France. We began in Paris in a rented British Vauxhall, which we reserved in New York, and headed down the highway towards the Belgian border. Although a funny noise seemed to be coming from the gas tank and some people on the way tried to catch our attention, we showed little concern, at first. The first to draw our attention to a problem was the gas station attendant across the Belgian side, where we stopped to fill up on gas. He pointed to the missing cap of the gas tank, which was the reason for the noise.

Although we initially thought to drive back to Paris and return the car, the attendant advised against this, since everything in France was closed on account of a national holiday. In the end, he found another cap and we were once again on our way.

But, this was just the beginning. When we stopped in Knokke, the Belgian beach resort where we expected to meet our relatives, the Perels (whom I had visited in 1957 on my way to the States), I was faced with another problem; the driver's door would not budge from the inside. So from there on, each time we chose to stop, my son Aaron Dovid went out and opened the driver's door from the outside. We were happy to meet our relatives Meir and Sola Perel, with whom we spent several hours. After a short rest in Brussels we continued on our way to Holland. But, apparently, the problem with the car door was not enough. While I was driving, the glove compartment door suddenly fell into Chava's lap, and for a finale, we soon discovered that the horn went on "strike" and fell silent.

Despite these disappointments, however, we made it to our destinations. Besides, it seemed to us that we had gone too far to return. We stopped in Amsterdam, Holland for two days and went sightseeing. First we visited the historic Tirado Synagogue, Beis Yaakov, named after the founder of the first recognized Jewish community of former Conversos (Marranos) in Holland. Yaakov Tirado arrived in Holland in 1593 heading a group of Portuguese Marranos. Four years later, the Marranos were officially permitted, for the first time, to live openly as Jews. To this day the Synagogue is lit with gas lights. The New York Spanish and Portuguese Synagogue was modeled after the one in Amsterdam. Then we went to see the dykes that prevent the ocean from flooding the low lands in Holland. Meanwhile, although we had been warned about pickpockets in Amsterdam, one of Chava's wigs was stolen from the car during the night.

Early next morning, we hit the highway and headed straight to Basel, Switzerland some 400 miles away, which was a long trip. We crossed into Switzerland through Basel, where the 1st Zionist Congress had gathered in 1897. From there we headed for Zurich, which is the financial center of Switzerland as well as a global banking center. I found the city extremely impressive with numerous attractions as well as stores, especially Bahnhof Street. From Zurich, we drove to the beautiful and awesome ski resort at Grindenwald, with a population of 3,736 residents, where we stayed for *Shabbos*. I had parked the car on a slope, but almost immediately, I noticed it was rolling backwards down the hill. I made a dash for the door and was barely able to slam my foot on the brakes in time.

One of the more amazing engineering achievements that we visited was the ice palace and the Eismeer train station, located 10,368 feet above the village of Grindenwald. The entire place is carved out of ice and rock.

After *Shabbos*, we began the return trip to Paris. Little did we expect the surprise that came as we reached the outskirts of Paris at the conclusion of our trip. The car, with all its problems, had made it all the way back, but at the entrance finally broke down. We then called the rental agency to pick up their junk.

In 1987, we chose the West Coast of the United States for our vacation. Together with another couple, we flew to Los Angeles, where we rented a car. We set out for the city of Las Vegas, which was to have been our first stop, in the early evening. As soon as we left, a heavy fog descended on the highway, making it impossible for us to drive. So we decided to park on the roadside and wait for the fog to lift. Trucks were racing past us in almost total darkness, but we stayed put.

It was not until early dawn that we were first able to get back on the highway. The trip to Vegas was about four hours, and by late morning we finally arrived. We then checked into a hotel where we davened and attended to the rest of our needs. By the afternoon, we had visited the casinos, some of which are beautifully designed like little palaces. It would have been unbecoming to visit this city without losing some money there, so we spent a short time playing in one of the casinos. The rest of the day we went touring the other parts of the city, which also had several kosher restaurants.

After Vegas, we headed for the Hoover Dam and the Grand Canyon, which are in close proximity to one another. The dam is a fascinating piece of engineering genius, the largest of its kind in the United States with its generators providing power to California, Nevada, and Arizona. The construction work, which was launched under the Roosevelt Administration during the great depression in

1931, was completed in 1936. The Grand Canyon, which we visited after the Hoover Dam, is 277 miles long, up to 18 miles wide and reaches a depth of over a mile. The Canyon is a gorge carved out by the Colorado River. After sleeping in a nearby motel, we continued towards our last destination, the border city of San Diego, which is on the coast of California near the Mexican border. It has several Orthodox Shuls, beautiful beaches, a famous Zoo, and an important United States naval base.

Three years later, in 1990, and on behalf of the Yeshiva of Flatbush, we flew to the Soviet Union, stopping at two cities, Moscow and Kishinev. These were the last years before the Soviet Union, under Chairman Gorbachev, broke up. At the airport the security officer opened one suitcase after the X-ray machine showed what he thought was a suspicious instrument. It was nothing more than a can opener, which he had never seen before. In Moscow, we visited the Yeshiva of *Rav* Steinsaltz, where we had the opportunity to speak with students, some of whom had come from far away cities in Siberia like Novogrod. On *Shabbos*, we davened at the famous Moscow Choral Synagogue, which dates back to the days of the Czars. This was followed by a *Kiddush* consisting of vodka and tomatoes. At one point we were amused when the *gabbai* approached my wife and advised her that she could not remain there without her hair being covered. She then pointed to her wig, which, to him, was a complete surprise. In Kishinev I delivered a lecture, in Yiddish, at a session chaired by Yaakov Fortune, a former *refusenik* who now lives in Monsey, New York. Present for the lecture was a large audience of some 600 Jews, most of them originally from Romania. The subject I chose was "The Rebirth of Israel," a very sensitive topic in those days in the Soviet Union, but was nevertheless openly advertised on the streets of Kishinev. While in Kishinev, both my wife and I gave classes in Torah to many whose only dream was *aliyah*. We also met the *shochet*.

From there we continued on to Rome, where a train took us north to a kosher hotel in a village located in the Italian Alps. We stayed there for the next ten days in the company of friends from Israel. The place was very scenic and the weather and food were great. In addition, every day one could join trips to many places

Red Square Moscow,   Advertisement for my lecture,
1990.   1990.

Class in Kishinev, 1990.

Opera House, Milan, Italy, 1990.

such as Austria, Serbia, and of course, to various towns in Italy. Together with our Israeli friends we visited several places, including the Italian cities of Venice and Milan. In Venice we toured the Jewish quarter where the first ghetto in history was opened in 1517. We also rode on a gondola. In Milan, which is one of the more attractive places in Italy, but half empty because it was summer, we stopped to see the famous opera house, La Scala.

The following day we crossed the border into Austria, a country that is highly picturesque, but which has a sad page in Jewish history. Austria is notorious as the birthplace of Hitler, and it is also the country that best supported his beastly ambitions, perhaps even more fiercely than the Germans themselves. When the Nazis humiliated the Jews of Vienna by forcing them to clean the streets with their toothbrushes, thousands of Austrians helped round up the Jews, and then stood by, laughed, and hailed the German action. Later we entered Bosnia, and toured many attractions such as the Sarajevo War Tunnel and some of the many waterfalls.

The following year, 1991, we vacationed on home territory once again, by flying to Hawaii. But first, I must give credit where credit is due. Almost every country we visited, Chabad was there to greet, accommodate and guide us with open arms. I called the Chabad office in Honolulu as soon as I landed there on a Thursday, to get the exact time of *Shabbos*. In response, the man at the other end gave me information, not only on *Shabbos*, but also assured me that although there is no regular *minyan* in Honolulu, should I need one he would organize it. Moreover, he also advised me on the availability of kosher packaged food with OU certification in some supermarkets.

Milan, Italy, 1990.

In Honolulu we toured Pearl Harbor. Since city bus travel was free, we went to many places on the island. After *Shabbos* we flew with Hawaiian Air to the island of Maui where we stayed at a hotel for about a week. The weather was great and the scenery was a dream.

In 1992, we joined Gesher Tours on a Scandinavian trip that included Finland, Sweden, Norway, and Denmark. First we flew from New York to Helsinki, Finland. Metropolitan Helsinki has a population of 1.4 million, and I found it to be one of the cleanest cities in the world. (It was later recognized by the British magazine *Monocle* as the most livable city in 2011.) We then boarded a big cruise ship to Stockholm, Sweden, where we arrived the next day. With a population of 2.2 million, the city consists of fourteen islands, and is considered the main center for corporate headquarters in the Nordic region. In 1950 the metro opened with its stations so well decorated that it has been called the longest art gallery in the world. Stockholm is best known for hosting the annual Nobel Prize ceremonies. We went on a tour of the city and vicinity and first stopped at the Palace. From there we continued to the Vasa Museum to see a 333-year-old Swedish warship that was salvaged from the sea, largely intact. Finally, we travelled to western Sweden where we visited one of the most interesting parks known as Sculpture Park.

Royal Palace, Stockholm, 1992.

The park has a very large collection of sculptures from all over the world on display. Although like much of Western Europe these days, Sweden, is among the fiercest supporters of Arab causes and hostility to Israel, it helped in the rescue of Danish Jewry from the Nazis.

From there, we continued by bus to Oslo, Norway, to see, among many other things, the glaciers. Many of the passengers on this bus tour felt insecure, as the bus climbed all the way to a mountain peak. The driver came around that peak, while engaged in a conversation with his girlfriend, with the steering wheel in one hand and the cell phone in the other. As we looked down at the villages below, they appeared as minute as if we were on a plane. It is, indeed, an un-forgettable experience to see the hundreds of glaciers as well as the numerous fjords. The bus tour that took us around, offered many scenic places where we stopped from time to time. Among these places, we also visited a large fisherman's market.

After Oslo we once again travelled on a big ship, this time to our last stop in Copenhagen, Denmark. In Copenhagen we stayed for *Shabbos*, which ended around two the next morning. So *maariv* was at ten p.m. but for *Havdalah* we woke up at two, since the following morning was *Tamuz* 17, a fast day. The following day,

Sculpture Park, western Sweden, 1992.

after an exciting adventure in the Scandinavian countries Finland Sweden, Norway and Denmark, we finally took our flight back to New York.

On another occasion we flew to Israel for a short vacation. We then proceeded to Switzerland on our way to Zermatt, the highest point in that country. Although the trip and the partial climb up the mountain were fascinating, the reception, once we got there, was in Swiss style. At first we took a four hour flight from Israel on Swiss Air to Zurich. We then boarded a train for another five hours to Zermatt, in southern Switzerland. After the train finally arrived, I called the hotel to notify them of our arrival, since cars are not permitted in the town, and the hotel was expected to pick up their guests. But the receptionist apologized and informed me that we lost the room, for which we had paid and made advance reservations, as we were supposed to have arrived at six, but it was already seven! This all happened after a four hour flight from Israel and another five hours by train from Zurich. In the end we found another hotel. We then checked in for three days and asked for a radio which did not come with the room, so as to keep up with the news. At check out, the receptionist gave us two bills, one for the accommodation,

Waterfall, Norway, 1992.

and the other for the electricity used for the radio! This was a very interesting visit and not only to the mountain peak.

In August 1994, we travelled to Romania for a two-week stay at a kosher hotel in Sinaia, a health resort in the Carpathian Mountains. The area is surrounded by scenic mountains, especially visible in the fall. Moreover, the place abounds with spas, gyms, athletic centers and various physical facilities. Many tourists from neighboring countries are attracted to Sinaia's popular ski resort. We felt like we were in the Swiss Alps, but without the very high Swiss price tag. Romania, as we then saw it, was still a very poor country.

That same year, my wife, Chava, finally retired from the library at the Yeshiva of Flatbush High School. She had worked in education since she was 21.

Our next vacation was to Alaska in 1995. Following an overbooking delay, for which we were well-compensated, we flew to Anchor-

Stockholm City Hall –
Venue of the Nobel Prize
banquet, 1992.

A Shul in Piatrz, Romania,
where the Baal Shem Tov *davened*,
1994.

Zermatt, 1993.

Sinaia, Romania, 1994.

age for a few days. The city has a Chabad *shul* but we were in for a surprise. Upon arriving at the *shul* on *Shabbos* morning, we saw the entire congregation sitting without shoes. At first I thought that perhaps this was their custom in Alaska. After prayers were over,

Shul interior Piatrz, Romania, 1994.

however, they explained, that the reason for that was because the carpet was new and there was snow outside!

The next day we went down to the harbor and took a boat ride. Although we had brought our own lunch, the food they served consisted of a bagel with tuna fish, sealed with the OU sign on it, and an apple. On this ocean cruise, we saw giant fish and seals as well as exotic birds.

On the following day, I was sitting on a bench in Anchorage reading a paper while Chava stepped into a boutique, when suddenly someone tapped me on the back. To my surprise it was Bobby Shenker, a family friend from New York, whose wife led a group on an Alaskan tour. Later we rented a car and headed up north on a trip of some 200 miles to Denali, where we joined an observation bus to watch bears and foxes. We were barely 120 miles from the North Pole. On the highway to Denali, with little traffic, I had the thrill of travelling some 90 miles per hour. At one point we passed a grizzly bear, standing on the side of the highway as if he were trying to hitch a ride. While on the bus at Denali, the driver stopped from time to time to point at some distant black spot which he identified as a Grizzly bear. I am sure I have seen them better on television. On the other hand, we saw some foxes that came up close to the bus. Truthfully, I was more fascinated by the landscape, which appeared in a blaze of many colors. As we said goodbye to Alaska, we noticed on the flight back that even during the month of August all the territory was completely snow-covered.

Our trip in August 1996 was not originally part of our plan, but it came about when we were bumped off a Northwest Airlines flight the year before because of overbooking. We had then made reservations for Alaska. When we arrived at Kennedy Airport, they had invited us to step aside and go with a later flight, to which we agreed. They later compensated us with two free round-trip tickets in the Continental U.S.

Consequently, we flew to Vancouver, a beautiful city with numerous attractions. After my *Zeide* the Modzitzer *Rebbe* died in 1947, the *Rebbetzin* Sarah Esther re-married and moved to this city. Greater Vancouver is the most populous place in Canada with some 2.4 million people. Because of its large film industry, it is also often referred to as Hollywood North. We went to see the salmon farming, the Capilano Suspension Bridge over which we walked, as well as the canyon lights and the galleries. This was then followed by a tour of downtown which we found to be very elegant.

From Vancouver we took a boat for a lengthy cruise to Seattle, Washington. Pike Place Market was the first attraction we visited. This is a very large farmers' market overlooking the bay area, which is open all year round and offers numerous products for sale. The Space Needle, another attraction in Seattle, is a landmark 605-foot observation tower in the Pacific Northwest. The Jewish community of Seattle is unique. Many of the people we met in *shul* are employed in the aircraft industry, primarily in Boeing. Many are either *baalei tshuva* or *geirim*. I also met the son of our *Rav*, Hillel David, with whom I daven on *Shabbos*, who runs a Kollel in Seattle.

On still another trip in 1997, we went to Prague, Czechoslovakia, a city with a very rich Jewish history. Especially notable was the famous Maharal, the (old *shul*) Altneuschul and one of the oldest Jewish cemeteries in Europe. We also visited the concentration camp at Theresienstadt, where many brothers and sisters lost their lives. For the Fast of *Tisha B'av* we were, once again, among many fasters at Chabad.

Finally, to conclude our trips in Europe, I will just mention our visit in 1999, to England. After a lengthy tour of London, including the Jewish district and all there was to see, and, indeed, there was an abundance of sight-seeing, we rented a car. We headed north, making sure that the car was on the opposite side than that in New York. The trip took us all the way to Scotland, with stops in some of the major towns, including, Edinburgh, Sheffield, Lancaster, and Gateshead, where we visited the famous Yeshiva.

On *Shabbos* we rested in the city of Edinburgh. *Shabbos* ended very late, about one o'clock in the morning. For a meaningful visit to England, three weeks is the required minimum.

The last trip we made, before my dear wife, Chava, fell ill, was in 2010, on a large Norwegian Cruise ship with close to 3000 passengers. Since an entire section of the ship was under kosher supervision, it was simply referred to as the Kosherica. It was a one-week cruise to the Caribbean Islands and Mexico, with provision of a full kosher kitchen, dining rooms, and places for prayer and learning. In addition, a team of some five famous cantors offered us daily entertainment, especially on *Shabbos*. Our cabin came with a porch and was first-class. The services were very good and very often it seemed that we were not on a ship but in a hotel.

On some of our travels, we were joined by our kids and a few were part of an organized group. Often we rented cars, but in Europe we occasionally took the trains, which are very modern and travel at very high speeds of over 150 miles per hour.

The most startling contrast between my earlier travels and later ones, however, was that while many of my early trips in life were part of an escape pattern from a tyrant and murderer, the later ones with my dear wife Chava, and sometimes with our children, were largely a fulfillment of a desire to see the world around us and the Jewish communities of past and present.

Conclusion

Retirement for my dear wife, Chava, and me, was a G-d given gift unrestricted in time. It enabled us to really enjoy the world around us after years of anxiety, tension and uncertainty as well as hard work. It opened the way for greater opportunities and closer engagement with our children, grandchildren and great grandchildren, delighting in their growth and achievements.

Some chose the great gift of Torah, spending many hours daily in *yeshiva*, while others have displayed great talent in advancing their professional careers, while still sharing their time with Torah.

For us, retirement has given us a chance for study, research and writing, as well as adventure in the world around us, including many Jewish communities. As seniors, G-d may have endowed us with better and more responsible insight and judgement of past and present. Publications such as משכן אברהם of my father's Torah, as well as the Modzitzer *Rebbe* and this autobiography, are some of the fruits of our retirement. Reflection on my past and my family opens our thoughts to many questions, not all of which have easy answers.

In conclusion, moreover, it is clearly indisputable that the growth and success of our family as that of many others, are clear proof that the monstrous ambition of Hitler and his contemporary sympathizers around the globe, *y"sh*, to destroy us, has with G-d's help, clearly failed.

We have, indeed also been able to take the one-time opportunity to see and observe post-Holocaust Europe, a continent which in the pre-war period had a thriving Jewish population of almost 10,000,000.[1] Many of these Jews were great rabbinical giants, scholarly thinkers, often well ahead of their time, and leaders in their fields of endeavor, who contributed their wealth of knowledge to the success of fellow Jews as well as to their non-Jewish neighbors.[2]

Unfortunately, Europe today, notwithstanding its beautiful and scenic attractions, is no longer a safe and hospitable place for Jews or even for non-Jews. In fact, advisories against travel to Europe seem to have increased in recent years. Wherever one goes, Hitler's footprints with a touch of Islamic extremism are easily felt and visible. In the not too distant future, we may hear names like Englanabad or Germanabad.

Unfortunately, our shared happiness that we so much valued with the family, especially in our retirement, suddenly and prematurely suffered an abrupt setback over three years ago, with the passing of my dear wife, Chava, my partner in life for the past 63 years.

Although my circle of friends, both here and in Israel, has an important place in my life, it is my children, grandchildren, and great-grandchildren, who are the bedrock of my pride and hope, and to whom I am indebted. It is primarily for them that I am writing this life story. Their tireless support does, indeed, keep me going, despite the devastating losses of the past. But last and not least, my beloved wife, Chava, *a"h*, her shared contributions, blessed with infinite wisdom and compassion, will forever be treasured by me and my children.

---

1. Malamat, *A History of the Jewish People*, p. *1063*. Hilberg, *The Destruction of the European Jews*, *670*.

2. Jacob R. Marcus, *The Jew in the Medieval World* (New York: Meridian Books and Philadelphia: JPS, 1960), p. 670.

Appendix

My Teacher's Diploma, 1951.

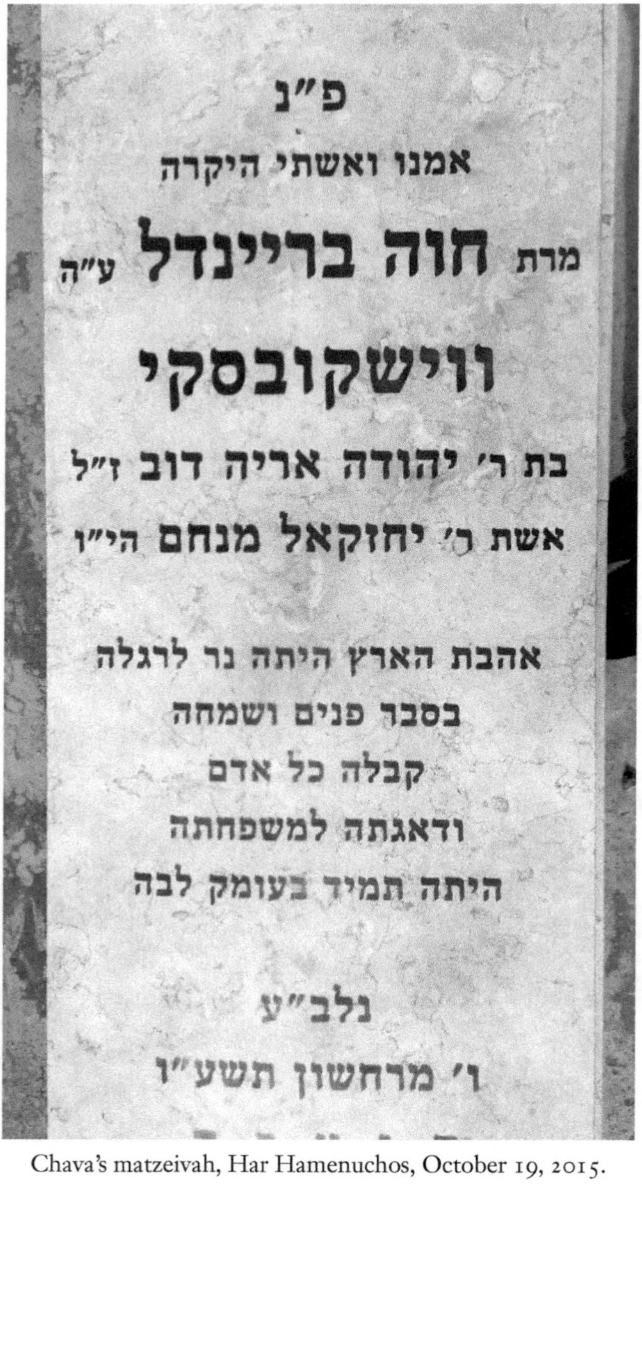

פ"נ

אמנו ואשתי היקרה

מרת **חוה ברײנדל** ע"ה

וױשקובסקי

בת ר' יהודה אריה דוב ז"ל

אשת ר' יחזקאל מנחם הי"ו

אהבת הארץ היתה נר לרגלה

בסבר פנים ושמחה

קבלה כל אדם

ודאגתה למשפחתה

היתה תמיד בעומק לבה

נלב"ע

ו' מרחשון תשע"ו

Chava's matzeivah, Har Hamenuchos, October 19, 2015.

Undelivered Letter from The *Rebbe* to my Mother, written in German
(Sent from New York to Warsaw and eventually returned), April 1941.

YESHIVA UNIVERSITY

500 West 185th Street / New York, N.Y. 10033 / (212) 568-8400

Mr. Chaskel Wyszkowski   June 2, 1971
1039 East 57th Street
Brooklyn, N.Y. 11234

Dear Mr. Wyszkowski:

    A review of your records shows that you have completed
all the requirements for the degree of Master of Arts with a major
in Modern Jewish History at the Bernard Revel Graduate School.

    Your name will therefore be presented to the Dean and
Faculty of this school for approval of this degree to be awarded
as of June 10, 1971.

                      Sincerely yours,

                      Larry Wachsman
                      Assistant Registrar

Form G10
(5/68)
cc:OSF
    Academic Offices

Notification of fulfillment of my Master of Arts degree requirements, 1971.

T.G.428.
Sch. C. 4417
5/1944.
This Telegram has been received subject to the Post and Telegraph Act and Regulations. The time received at this office is shown at the end of the message.
COMMONWEALTH OF AUSTRALIA.
POSTMASTER-GENERAL'S DEPARTMENT.
TELEGRAM
The date stamp indicates the date of reception and lodgment also, unless an earlier date is shown after the time of lodgment.
Office of Origin. No. of Words. Time of Lodgment.

2 VIA CABLE 1096 JERUSALEM 79 10 1025

NLT ...RABBI A WYSHKOVSKY

109 MC PHERRON ST MELBOURNE4

RABBI YECHIEL YOSHUAH RABBINOWITCH WIFE AND SON HERSCHEL STILL IN
TURKESTAN RUSSIA STOP HIS GOAL IS PALESTINE STOP WE WILL DO ALL
NECESSARY TO OBTAIN IMMIGRATION CERTIFICATE WE ARE APPOINTING HIM
DIRECTOR OF STUDIES OF THE ___ ___ L COLLEGE YESHIVATH DARKEI
TSHUVAH TELEAVIV UNDER THE RA___ MUNKATCH STOP HIS ECONOMIC

T.G.428.
Sch. C. 4417
5/1944.
This Telegram has been received subject to the Post and Telegraph Act and Regulations. The time received at this office is shown at the end of the message.
COMMONWEALTH OF AUSTRALIA.
POSTMASTER-GENERAL'S DEPARTMENT.
TELEGRAM
The date stamp indicates the date of reception and lodgment also, unless an earlier date is shown after the time of lodgment.
Office of Origin. No. of Words. Time of Lodgment. No.

FUTURE SECURED STOP PRAY ENDEAVOUR UTMOST GET PERMIT ENTRY AUSTRALIA
TEMPORARY UNTIL IMMIGRATION CERTIFICATE PALESTINE OBTAINED THANKS
GREETINGS ... CHIEFRABBI HERZOG

109 MC PHERRON)

Telegram from Harav Herzog, 1945.

YESHIVA UNIVERSITY

DUPLICATE

500 West 185th Street / New York, N.Y. 10033 / (212) 568-8400

Dr. Chaskel Wyszkowski
1274 East 57 th Street   February 12, 1979
Brooklyn, New York 11234

A review of your records shows that you have completed all the
requirements for the degree of Doctor of Philosophy with a major in
Jewish History at the Bernard Revel Graduate School.

Your name will therefore be presented to the Dean and Faculty of
this school for approval of this degree to be awarded as of January 31, 1979

Sincerely yours,

Larry Wachsman
Assistant Registrar

Ken Blackstein
Assistant to the Registrar

Form G10.3
(9/73)
cc: OSF
    Academic Offices

Notification of approval for my doctoral degree (Ph.D), 1979.

מדינת ישראל
משרד החנוך והתרבות

א ג ף ה ח נ ו ך
ירושלים
ת. ד. 7001 · טלפון 1271

בתשובה נא לציין:
מספר _____ 86/P
תאריך _____ י״ס באייר תש״י

לכבוד

כב׳ גברת חוה

נ. ג.

הננו מאשרים בזה, שלמדת וסיימת את הקורס לגננות שנערך מטעם

אגף החנוך ע״י ביהמ״ד לגננות "תלפיות"

ב חורף תש״י ועל סמך זה נתנת לך הרשות להורות בגן־ילדים.

עם זה הננו להודיעך, שמסרנו לידיעת הבחינות למורים את כל הפרטים על

השכלתך ואת הערכת מורי הקורס על הכשרתך ועבודתך המעשית, והיא תקבע את

מעמדך לגבי בחינות המלואים בהתאם לתקנות.

בכבוד רב

ד״ר ב. בן־יהודה
המנהל

Chava's, *a"h*, certification from the Department of Education course
for Kindergarten Teachers, 1950.

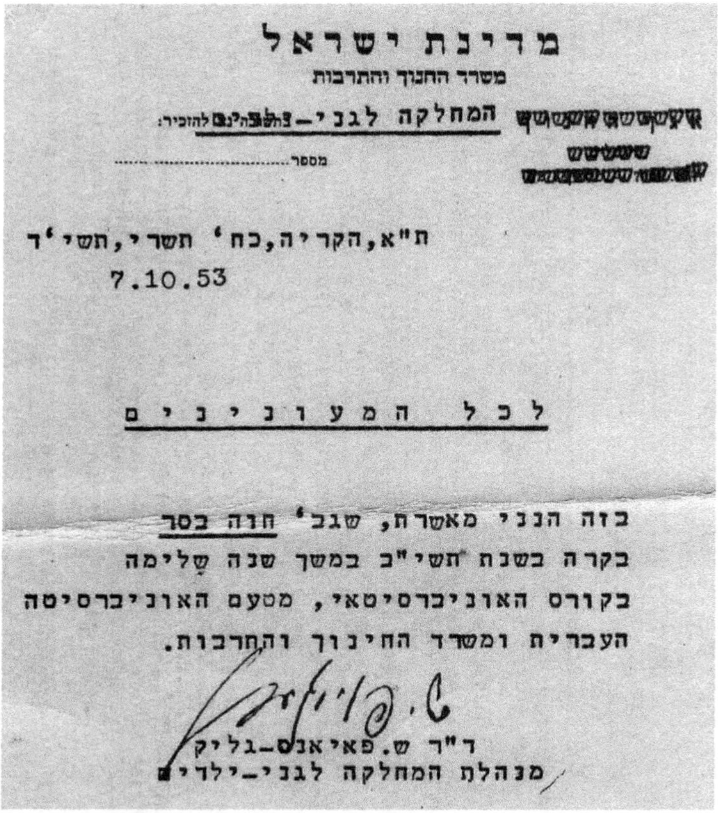

מדינת ישראל

משרד החנוך והתרבות

המחלקה לגני ‏ ‏—‎ להזכיר:

מספר ....

ח"א, הקריה, כח' תשרי, תשי"ד
7.10.53

ל כ ל ה מ ע ו נ י י ם

בזה הנני מאשרת, שגב' חוה בסר
בקרה בשנת תשי"ב במשך שנה שלימה
בקורס האוניברסיטאי, מטעם האוניברסיטה
העברית ומשרד החינוך והתרבות.

ד"ר ש. פאיאנס-גליק
מנהלת המחלקה לגני-ילדים

A Hebrew University Course for Kindergarten Principals
completed by Chava, *a"h*, 1953.

LEGATION OF JAPAN

BRANCH CHANCELLERY
MELBOURNE, C.I.

7th August, 1941.

My dear Prime Minister,

I desire to acknowledge the receipt, with
many thanks, of your telegram of today's date, inform-
ing me, in reply to my letter of yesterday regarding
the cargo by the s.s. "Kasima Maru", that the
Commonwealth Government is prepared to allow the un-
loading of the cargo, the proceeds to be held in escrow
and used for payment for allowable exports under contract.　This information has been duly conveyed to
the Japanese Government.

I hasten to inform you that I have just
received advice from the Agents of the Nippon Yusen
Kaisha that the above-named vessel will arrive at
Sydney at approximately 8 a.m. on Saturday next, the
9th instant.

Yours faithfully,

Japanese Minister.

COPY TO MIN. & DEPT. T. & C. (PREV. CORRES.)
MIN. & DEPT. COMMERCE　　"　　"

The Rt. Hon. R. G.Menzies, K.C.,
　　Prime Minister,
　　　　Commonwealth of Australia,
　　　　　　Commonwealth Offices,
　　　　　　　　Treasury Gardens,
　　　　　　　　　MELBOURNE.

Japanese Consul in Australia thanks the government for allowing to
unload Japanese Cargo, 1941.

TELEPHONE : CANBERRA 551.

COMMONWEALTH OF AUSTRALIA.

CABLE AND TELEGRAPHIC ADDRESS:
"TRACUSTOMS," CANBERRA.

PLEASE ADDRESS REPLY TO
"THE COMPTROLLER-GENERAL."
AND QUOTE

T. & C._____/_____

DEPARTMENT OF TRADE AND CUSTOMS,
CANBERRA, A.C.T.

12th August, 1941

11694

Immediate

MEMORANDUM:

It is desired that a cablegram in the following terms be forwarded to the Secretary of State for Dominion Affairs, London:

526/

"Your telegram 405 to your High Commissioner conveying message to Central Wool Committee from Lord Essendon.

Commonwealth Government made arrangement with Japanese Legation here that if Kasima Maru which had left Japan with cargo for Australia before publication of freezing order were to discharge cargo in Australia exports of approved goods equal in value to the value of imports less costs incurred in servicing vessel would be permitted.

In view of terms of your telegram 519 dated 28th July Commonwealth Government advised Japanese Legation that raw wool would be made available to the value of the imported cargo less ship's expenses. In addition permission would also be given for the loading of the 8,534 bales of wool which had been paid for in London before freezing of Japanese funds.

Japanese Legation have now advised that in addition to the 8,534 bales of wool they desire to export an additional 4,000 bales of wool and 2,000 tons of wheaten flour. Value of the additional wool and flour is much less than cargo landed off Kasima Maru. Question of additional exports for balance of value of inward cargo will be considered when further request is received from Japanese Legation.

So far as the 4,000 bales of wool are concerned the arrangement will of course result in payment being received in Australia instead of in sterling in London but we presume this will not be a material factor in view of the large remittances which are regularly made to the credit of the Central Wool Committee.

The Secretary,
  Prime Minister's Department,
  CANBERRA.   A.C.T.

Typed

P.T.O.

Declassified documents pertaining to *Kasima Maru, 1941*.

Letter from the Lubavitcher *Rebbe* to my father in Australia, 1942.

My application for Australian (British) citizenship, 1948.

Bibliography

PRIMARY SOURCES

TAUB, SHAUL YEDIDYA ELOZOR. Letters from Otwock. Vilna, and New York, 1930–1946 (unpublished).

WYSZKOWSKI, MALKA. Letters from Ghetto Warsaw, 1939–1941 (unpublished).

WYSZKOWSKI, MOSHE. Letters from New York, 1941–1949 (unpublished).

קאפעל, יעקב עמנואל. ספר אמת ליעקב. נערך ע"י ישראל קאפל. בני ברק: שרגא זלמנוב, תשס"ח [2007]

SECONDARY SOURCES

1. BOOKS

ALFASI, YITZCHAK. *Jewish Glimpses of Warsaw*. New York: CIS, 1992.

BERKMAN, TED. *Sabra: The Story of the Men and Women behind the Guns of Israel*. New York: Harper and Row, 1967.

ELBOGEN, ISMAR. *A Century of Jewish Life*. Philadelphia: JPS, 1966.

FINKELSTEIN, LOUIS, ED. *The Jews*. New York: Schocken, 1970.

GILBERT, MARTIN. *The Holocaust*. New York: Holt, Reinhart and Winston, 1985.

GORR, SHMUEL. "From Kelme to Melbourne." *Yiddishkeit* (Tammuz 1986): 2–9, (Tishrei 1987): 11–19.

GREENE, RON. *Visas for Freedom: The Remarkable Story of Chiune and Yukika Sugihara*. Kovno: Sugihara Family Foundation, 1995–96.

HAVIN, J. *Jewish Carlton Comes to Life*. Melbourne: Oz Tora [Block Archive], 2007.

HILBERG, RAUL. *The Destruction of the European Jews*. New York: Quadrangle Books, 1973.

KANZ, SHIMON. *Otwock-Korchev, Memorial Book*. Tel Aviv, 1968.

KLAPERMAN, GILBERT. *The Story of Yeshiva University*. Toronto: Macmillan, 1969.

KOTSUJI, ABRAHAM. *From Tokyo to Jerusalem*. New York: Geis Associates, 1964.

KRANZLER, DAVID. *The Japanese, Nazis and Jews*. Hoboken, NJ: Ktav, 1988.

LAQUEUR, WALTER. *A History of Zionism*. New York: Holt, Rinehart and Winston, 1972.

LEVIN, NORA. *The Holocaust. The Destruction of European Jewry*. New York: Crowell, 1978.

MAHLER, RAPHAEL. *The Jews in Poland Between Two World Wars* (Hebrew). Tel Aviv: Dvir, 1968.

MALAMAT, A. et al. *A History of the Jewish People*. Edited by H. H. Ben Sasson. Cambridge, MA: Harvard University Press, 1976.

MANDELBAUM, DAVID A. *From Lublin to Shanghai*. New York: Mesorah, 2012.

MARCUS, JACOB. R., *The Jew in the Medieval World*. New York: Meridian Books and Philadelphia: JPS, 1960.

MENDES-FLOHR, PAUL AND JEHUDA REINHARZ, EDS. *The Jew in the Modern World. A Documentary History*. New York: Oxford University Press, 1995.

PARZEN, HERBERT. *The Hebrew University 1925–1935*. New York: Ktav, 1974.

PHILLIPS, EDWARD, ED. *Flight and Rescue*. Washington, DC: The Holocaust Museum, 2001.

ROTH, LEON. *The Hebrew University and Its Place in the Modern World*. London: Jewish Historical Society of England, 1945.

ROTHKOFF, AARON. *Bernard Revel: Builder of American Jewish Orthodoxy*. Philadelphia: JPS, 1972.

SACHAR, HOWARD M. *The Course of Modern Jewish History*. New York: Vintage Books, 1990.

TALMON, YONINA. *Family and Community in the Kibbutz.* Cambridge, MA: Harvard University Press, 1972.

TOKAYER, MARVIN. *The Fugu Plan.* New York: Weatherhill, 1979.

WYSZKOWSKI, CHARLES (CHASKEL). *A Community in Conflict: American Jewry During the Great European Immigration.* New York: University Press of America, 1991.

WYSZKOWSKI, CHASKEL. *The Modzitzer Rebbe.* New York: Chaskel Wyszkowski, 2010.

ZAKON, NACHMAN. *The Jewish Experience: 2000 Years.* Brooklyn, NY: Shaar Press, 2002.

אורליאן, מאיר. הקבוץ הדתי והתפתחותו, תל-אביב: הקיבוץ הדתי, תש"ו.

גלבר, יואב. המאבק לצבא עברי (תולדות ההתנדבות, כרך ב'). ירושלים: יד יצחק בן צבי.

ווישקובסקי, אברהם. משכן אברהם, ירושלים: אות הזהב, 2006.

וייצמן, חיים. האוניברסיטה העברית בירושלים: כ"ה שנה. ירושלים, תש"י.

ויסברוד-הלחמי, יעקב דוד. אהל יוסף: בית אמשינאוו, תל אביב: אגודת "אהל יוסף", תשע"ד.

טאוב, רב ישראל דוד. יד יחזקאל. נערך ונסדר ע"י יחזקאל מקוזמיר זצוק"ל ושמואל אליהו מזוואלין זצוק"ל. ניו יורק: מכון אשי ישראל, תשע"ב.

טאוב, הרב ישראל דוד. ישא ברכה. נערך ונסדר ע"י שאול ידידיה אלעזר זצוק"ל. ניו יורק: מכון אשי ישראל, תשע"ג.

טאוב, הרב ישראל דוד. דברי ישראל. נערך ונסדר ע"י. ישראל זצוק"ל. ניו יורק: מכון אשי ישראל, תשע"ו.

לבל, אהובה. הציונות הדתית, הוצאת אמי"ת, 1990, ירושלים.

2. NEWSPAPERS

Der Moment (Warsaw), June 7, 1928 (Yiddish).

Unzer Express (Warsaw), June 7, 1928 (Yiddish).

Advocate (Melbourne, Australia), August 11, 1941.

Argus (Melbourne, Australia), August 11, 1941.

Sydney Morning Herald, August 1, 1941.

Index